Recovery the Native Way

A Client Reader

Recovery the Native Way

A Client Reader

by

Alf H. Walle
Ilisagvik College Barrow, Alaska

Information Age Publishing, Inc.
Charlotte, North Carolina • www.infoagepub.com

ISBN 13: 978-1-60752-014-6

Printed in the United States of America

Dedication

This book is dedicated to those who seek to develop strategies of therapy that are aimed toward the special needs of Native people who seek to use their cultures, heritage, and traditions as tools of recovery.

CONTENTS

Preface

This book is written in the belief that many Native substance abusers suffer because their cultural heritage is being swept away or because they have lost contact with it. While Alcoholics Anonymous and Narcotics Anonymous provide wonderful leadership to millions of people, they do not deal with the pain that can arise when cultures weaken and die or when people are cut off from their heritage.

While not seeking to replace tools of recovery, such as Alcoholics Anonymous and Narcotics Anonymous, this book deals with the fact that people often lose the ability to cope when their cultures are under attack. The resulting pain can lead to substance abusers. If strengthened, however, the traditions of a people can help people regain their sobriety.

The example of Handsome Lake, a Native leader who lived many years ago, demonstrates the power of tradition. Handsome Lake was an alcoholic near death who, at the last possible moment, regained his sobriety and invented a method that helped the Iroquois people overcome their alcoholism and restore their culture. This strategy was made up of two parts (1) reaffirming and strengthening the culture and (2) living a sober life while undoing past wrongs.

This book is written to show how Handsome Lake's inspirational example can help today's Native people who seek recovery from substance abuse.

Prologue to Part 1
A Puzzling Situation

Nobody knows for sure why some people become alcoholics or substance abusers while others do not. In this section you will begin to think about why some of your friends may be able to safely enjoy a drink or two while you cannot.

In Exercise 1, you will look at the short story "The Man Without a Country" because it shows that people can become unhappy when they lose touch with their heritage and their culture. You will then be asked to think about the possibility that you, in some way, might have been cut off from your heritage and suffered as a result.

In Exercise 2, you will think about your Native heritage. On the one hand, many different Native cultures exist. Just as Swedes and Southern Italians are very different, profound differences exist between various Natives peoples. In recent years, however,

Native people are beginning to band together like never before because they often face similar pressures. In Exercise 2, you will consider these issues and how they relate to your life.

In Exercise 3, you will ask "Why me? Why do I have a problem with alcohol or drugs when others do not?" In doing so, you will consider some of the popular theories regarding Native people, alcoholism, and substance abuse. In general, two basic sets of theories exist. One relates Native alcoholism to biological causes while the other points to social and cultural pressures that trigger alcoholic drinking and substance abuse.

These exercises should help you develop a better understanding of yourself and, perhaps, why you are a substance abuser. This is an excellent first step to recovery.

Chapter 1

The Man Without a Country

The story "The Man without a Country" is used in order to emphasize the fact that when people deny or ignore their heritage, the results are often devastating. Having made this point, we will discuss how the decline of Native Cultures can trigger trauma and dysfunction.

One of the most famous lessons ever told is found in a short story entitled "The Man Without a Country." When I was in high school, everybody had to read it. Maybe you did too.

School teachers probably required the story in order to help us develop feelings of patriotism. But the story does more than that. "The Man Without a Country" also helps us to understand the nature of suffering is and what can cause it. People often find it easy to forget that much misery and sorrow is created by spiritual pain, not merely by physical hurt. "The Hero Without a Country" reminds us of that truth.

The story also suggests that on many occasions people might not immediately realize what, in the long run, will hurt them. As a result, they often focus life and death issues and downplay everything else.

"The Man Without a Country" deals with pain and unhappiness that can easily be ignored. As a result, the story has a special message for Native people. Even though they may enjoy the physical comforts, they may live in a world that is changing so quickly that they must endure the loss of their heritage, culture, and way of life. This can cause pain that is easily ignored.

THE STORY

The plot of "The Man Without a Country" is easily told. The story opens at the trial for a man who has been accused of treason. He has been found guilty and will probably be put to death.

As the defendant's fear rises, so does his anger. And at some point he begins bad-mouthing the judge. He goes on to say that he hates his country and wishes he never had to deal with it or see it again.

The judge givers his verdict. The defendant will remain in custody for the rest of his life, typically on board a ship sailing the high seas. He will be free to move about. All of his needs will be taken care of. He will live a normal and comfortable life in every way except he will never see his country again. And he will not even be allowed to hear about it.

The prisoner is overjoyed to have received such a lenient sentence.

The rest of the story shows how our hero's attitude changes as, day by day and year by year, the punishment drags on. Although nobody hurts him in any physical way and although all his needs are satisfied, pain begins to take hold of him because he is forever cut off from his people. Many years later, after the prisoner dies, a homemade American flag is found among his belongings and the writings in his notebooks that indicate the degree to which he had attempted to use the small bits of information he gained, here and there, to understand what was happening back home. He dies isolated and alone.

Although, at first, the man without a country didn't realize the sorrow and hurt that his punishment would cause, he found out that losing his culture and heritage was a terrible ordeal. The punishment was worse than execution.

THE MESSAGE

One important message of this story is that people are not merely animals living instinctively, because they have cultures and traditions. They often feel pain when their heritage is denied them or if it rapidly weakens or changes. Even when people do not consciously realize that their heritage is important to them, it can still exert a powerful force. When their culture is not available as a strong and vital force, people often suffer terribly.

An important theme of "The Man Without a Country" is that our hero does not immediately realize that this is a horrible and painful fate. The message of the story is that people are linked to their culture and to their heritage if they realize it or not. Being denied their heritage can be terribly painful to people.

I don't recall if the story tells us if the man without a country is allowed to visit the ship's rum-barrel on a regular basis or not. Judging from the remorse and pain he felt, I wouldn't be surprised if, over time, he developed a bad drinking habit.

WHAT ABOUT YOU?

I doubt that you have been found guilty of treason and forced to sail the high seas out of eyesight of your homeland for the rest of your life.

But people can be denied their culture and their heritage in numerous ways. Many Native people, for example, find themselves in a situation where, for one reason or another, they can no longer connect with their culture, their heritage, and their people.

For one thing, Native cultures are often weakened by diseases and changes brought by outside contact. People often feel great pain when their culture and society are swept away. I remember a book named *Ishi* that was written by a woman named Theodore Kroeber. Ishi was the last member of his tribe. Everybody else was dead. Nobody but Ishi remembered his way of life. There were no other members of the tribe for him to talk to. Nobody but Ishi knew of or cared about his Gods. Nobody else remembered the stories of his people or his way of life. Everything and everybody else was gone forever. Think of the pain he must have felt and how terribly alone he must have been.

The story of Ishi, however, ends on a positive note. Being the last member of his tribe, he dedicated himself to recording everything he could about his heritage. Although his culture was physically dead, he spent his remaining years preserving his heritage. And he did a wonderful job. Although terribly hurt by his loneliness, he found comfort by leaving a legacy for future generations. As a result, he lived a useful and constructive life; although I am sure he had moments of sadness and loneliness.

For our purposes, it is useful to compare the man without the country with Ishi, the last member of his tribe. Both found that their world was dead to them. Both suffered terribly as a result. Both found comfort in gathering and preserving whatever was left to them, reconstructing to the best of their ability what had been lost.

What about you? Many Native people have suffered great pain because their culture became so weakened it no longer worked for them. Many Native people have turned to substance abuse for just that reason.

In other cases, the culture may remain, but some Native people are unable to embrace it. Many people have had their personal heritage stripped away. At one time, Native students were sent to boarding schools where teachers made every effort to destroy their Native traditions. Students were made to feel ashamed of their culture and they were severely punished for speaking their language or practicing the ways of their people. When they completed school, many of the graduates of the boarding schools were no longer Natives, but they weren't White either.

A number of those who attended the boarding schools have personally told me that being caught between two worlds was a terribly painful experience. And some have speculated that the resulting confusion and sorrow triggered their alcoholism. On a positive note, some of these same people have also told me that by embracing their culture they were able to find a worthwhile and fulfilling recovery.

Some Native people live far removed from their heritage. Little by little and day by day, many of these people lose a meaningful connection with their culture. Some Native people come to think of themselves are "mainstream" Americans who just happen to possess Native blood. In reality, these people might not realize how important their culture is and feel pain when it is denied them.

Thus, there are a wide variety of ways in which people can become distanced from their heritage. And like Ishi and the man without a country, Native people are often hurt when this happens. But the good news is that Ishi returned to health by embracing his heritage. This was true even though his culture was dead. Your culture may possess the tools that you need to build a strong recovery.

THE FULL MEASURE OF WHO YOU ARE

People are social creatures and they are members of their culture. When that heritage is denied, the results are often terribly hurtful. When people deny their pain, its power may build up silently. Such a situation can leave people completely unprotected because when people don't realize an enemy is lurking, they cannot defend themselves. Many Native people have failed to understand how much they had been hurt because their culture was denied them and became substance abusers as a result.

To what extent are you a member of your culture? To what extent are you able to embrace that heritage in a positive and joyous way? I'm not asking you for any answer right now. I'm merely stating some questions you might want to ask yourself.

Remember that Native people have often become substance abusers because their culture traditions were unable to help them.

HOW DO PEOPLE DEAL WITH LOSS?

Native people have suffered many losses. This is true in North America and among other Native people from around the world. And these losses and the tragedies that accompany them often occur generation after generation, without a break. In many cases, a general feeling of hopelessness surrounds people with a pain that is never relieved.

How do people deal with such losses? Alcoholic drinking and substance abuse is a common response. What losses do you consciously feel? Are there any loses that might be impacting you even though you don't dwell upon them? Is it possible that some of these silent and invisible losses triggering your substance abuse? If so, you won't be the first.

ONWARD FROM HERE

The purpose of this book is to remind you that the pain caused by not being able to embrace your heritage and our culture can lead to substance abuse. This is the bad news.

The good news is that your heritage may be able to help you develop the strength you need for a strong and vital recovery. Thus, the cause of your weakness can also give you strength.

In order to present this point, I will rely upon the historic example of Handsome Lake, a Native alcoholic who returned to sobriety. After gaining his recovery, furthermore, Handsome Lake developed a method of recovery that included rebuilding the strength and health of his culture. We will discuss this inspiring example of recovery in the hope that it will encourage you to follow your own path of sobriety.

Handsome Lake's path towards sobriety and cultural renewal can be employed by members of many Native cultures and it members because it is based upon the fact that healing can result if people accept and embrace who they really are. This is exactly the kind of therapy and self-help that many Native substance abusers need.

In the pages that follow, Handsome Lake's program of recovery is updated and presented in a way that you can embrace. Perhaps his vision of hope and cultural renewal is what you need to recovery.

Chapter 2

A Proud Tradition

An appreciative overview of the cultural diversity of Native North Americans and their struggles is presented. Similarities and differences between different Native American cultures are discussed. Parallels between Native Americans and other Native peoples throughout the world are analyzed in order to expand the range of the book.

Often thinking in terms of the stereotypes presented in cowboy movies, many people assume that all Native North Americans are pretty much the same. Nothing could be further from the truth. Just as Europeans from southern Italy and those of Scandinavia are very different, Native North Americans show similar variations. Besides American Indians, various Native Alaskan groups, such as the Yupik and the Inupiaq, are culturally and biologically distinct.

For many years, these differences kept Native North Americans from cooperating with each other for their mutual benefit. White intruders often formed alliances with one Native community in order to subdue another. If the Whites had not been able to do so, they probably would have been unable to conquer North America, at least not until repeating rifles became available.

In spite of these age-old rivalries, many Native American societies are now cooperating because they realize that doing so is in their mutual interest. Even though specific groups remain proud of their heritage, they increasingly support and collaborate with each other, as well as possessing a sense of a shared identity.

This chapter provides a brief overview of various Native North American cultures and their distinctiveness. It also discussed hardships that can trigger dysfunctional behavior such as substance abuse. A comparison of Native North Americans with other groups, such as Native Hawaiians and the

Maori of New Zealand, demonstrate how all have been subjected to similar experiences. These non American Native groups can also benefit from the tools that this book offers.

NATIVE AMERICANS: WHO ARE THEY?

When Christopher Columbus "discovered" America in 1492, he met descendants of the original settlers who, in prehistoric times, had traveled across the land bridge that once connected Siberia and Alaska (or arrived by a different route). Eventually, these pioneers settled both North and South America and adjusted themselves and their cultures to their environments.

The coming of White people triggered powerful and often hurtful changes. Even when the Whites were friendly, they brought European diseases that killed untold numbers of Native people. These unexpected plagues left Native cultures in a state of pain, suffering, and confusion. Alcoholic drinking among the survivors often resulted (Napoleon, 1996.)

White intruders, furthermore, often enslaved or killed off the local inhabitants. During the first half of the nineteenth century, Native people East of the Mississippi River were sent into exile. After the United States Civil War (1861-65), White settlers started moving West in large numbers. As a result of this migration, more and more Native people were denied their land and confined to reservations. This situation, although hurtful, might not have been unbearable to those who already lived in villages, but it was a terrible hardship to those who earned a living by traveling from place to place in search of food and did not live in one place.

While Alaska was spared the horrors of being conquered, disease, famine, and a weakening of traditional cultures had a hurtful effect.

In spite of hardship, the cultures of many Native North Americans continue to be strong. Today, approximately one third of Native Americans live on reservations, while about one half resides in urban areas (that are often close to reservations). As with other groups within American society, some Native people treasure the old ways and want to preserve them while other members of the same culture favor modernization and economic development.

We can gain insights from looking at *Goodbye Columbus* a novel by Philip Roth. It tells the story of how different Jewish-American immigrants and their families adjusted to the United States. Some of these Jews treasure their heritage and the close-knit community it makes possible. These people are saddened when the younger generation ignores or does not emphasize its ethnic and religious traditions. Other people, while proud of their religion and their culture, think of themselves primarily as "Americans." They don't want to be held back by an identity that limits their opportunities. I have seen a similar pattern within several Native Americans communities. One group looks towards its heritage and traditions while others are more interested in the outside world and the opportunities to be found there.

SUBGROUPS AND THEIR SIGNIFICANCE

Even though facing hardships for many years, many Native cultures survive in North America. Recognized culture areas of the Native people of North America include the Southwest, the Eastern Woodlands, the Southeast, the Plains, the California-Intermountain region, the Plateau, the Pacific Northwest Coast, the Subarctic, and the Arctic. Let's consider their differences and achievements.

THE SOUTHWESTERN CULTURAL AREA

The so-called "four corners" region of Arizona, Utah, New Mexico, and Colorado, and extending into Mexico is the home of the Southwestern cultural area. This is where we find the awe inspiring "cliff dwellings," perhaps the most impressive structures of the prehistoric United States.

Many of these people were farmers who grew corn and lived in towns. They can be viewed as a success story since descendants of this cultural tradition (such as Pima and Papago (now Tohono O'Odham) continue to be strong and preserve their way of life.

Similar cultures once existed among the Anasazi people to the north but after 1275 A.D. severe droughts caused many regions to be abandoned. Relocating to the Rio Grande River, they were conquered by the Spanish and were eventually dominated the United States. Although, their traditional religion and traditions were long outlawed, the people secretly kept them alive and they still survive today. Approximately 20 such towns still exist.

The Navaho are relative new comers to the area, arriving as hunters in the 1400s. The Navaho speak an Athabascan language and are directly related to the Athabascan tribes of interior Alaska. They learned how to farm from their neighbors and eventually settled in towns. The Apache, the last to arrive, lived a nomadic way of life until forced to live on reservations.

People from this area have every reason to be proud of their heritage. The people built many important buildings, invented ways to irrigate their farmland, and facing great obstacles, they preserved their cultures.

THE EASTERN WOODLAND CULTURAL AREA

The Eastern part of North America, located between North Carolina in the south up into Canada, in the North, is home of the Eastern Woodlands cultural area. This was a region of vast forests. The land was shared by both farmers who lived in small towns and by hunters and gathers that moved around following the seasons.

The Iroquois are among the best-known Woodland people. They lived in villages. To this day, the Iroquois are a vital force in New York State and the Province of

Ontario. The Algonquian-speaking peoples, in contrast, were hunters and gathers. Eventually the Iroquois overpowered the Algonquian people and their power declined, although they and their cultures still exist.

There is much to admire in these people. The political organization of the Iroquois has often been praised. And the men of the region were brave and feared warriors.

THE SOUTHEAST CULTURAL AREA

The Southeast cultural area ranges from the Gulf of Mexico on the south to the Eastern Woodlands region on the north and extends from the Atlantic Ocean to central Texas. The region supported large farming communities when Hernando De Soto, the first European to visit the area, arrived. Diseases brought by the Spanish, however, caused these people to quickly decline.

Best known today are the Cherokee, the Choctaw, the Chickasaw, the Creek, and the Seminole. After the American Revolution and before the Civil War, these highly civilized nations were crushed by the United States. In a shameful example of arrogance, Andrew Jackson forced the Cherokee to move to what is now Oklahoma in an infamous forced migration known as "the trail of tears."

The Natchez was a particularly impressive culture but it was completely destroyed by Europeans in the eighteenth century. Today, the Natchez are considered to be extinct as a culture, although, genetically, some descendants of the Natchez may survive. Because archaeologists point to their achievements, we look with admiration at the Natchez, although most of their cultural heritage is gone.

THE PLAINS CULTURAL AREA

The Great Plains consists of grasslands ranging from central Canada to Mexico and from the Midwest westward to the Rocky Mountains. The people living in the plains relied heavily upon buffalo. As a result, their way of life ended when the herds were destroyed by the Whites in the 1880s. The people of the plains preferred to live in small nomadic bands that followed the moving herds. A few towns existed, but they were not typical.

The image of "the American Indian" that exists in the public eye is largely based on the plains people. They, for example, were the people who originally wore long feather headdress, smoked peace pipes, and lived in tepees.

The plains people were feared warriors. Not only were they brave, they also developed important tactics for warfare that have survived to this day and are even taught at military colleges such as West Point.

THE CALIFORNIA INTERMOUNTAIN CULTURAL AREA

The mountainous region of Utah, Nevada, and California is a land of pine forests, grasslands, and valleys. For thousands of years, the people living there were left alone to create a way of life that was based upon hunting, fishing, and gathering pine nuts and other wild grains. Appearing backward at first glance, their knowledge of the environment was very sophisticated. The artistry of their basket making and other crafts, furthermore, demonstrates both skill and an artistic eye.

THE PLATEAU CULTURAL AREA

Parts of Idaho, Oregon, Washington, Montana, and the adjacent Canadian provinces of Alberta and British Columbia are a world of evergreen forests and grassy valleys. The people lived by hunting and gathering. The annual salmon run was especially important and large quantities of fish were dried and eaten during the winter.

Perhaps the most famous Plateau people are the Nez Percé (the name derives from a French description of their pierced noses (Nez Pere means "pierced nose")). The Nez Perce were a prosperous tribe that lived by salmon fishing. They eventually gained horseback riding skills that were used to supplement their income. Many people, Native and non-Native alike, are inspired by Chief Joseph who, after fighting a brilliant military campaign, was stalled by a snowstorm and captured in 1877. His speeches are especially treasured.

THE PACIFIC NORTHWEST COAST CULTURAL AREA

The Pacific coast of North America is a narrow strip of fertile land lying between the sea and the mountains. The area is rich in salmon and sea mammals and the land provides sheep, goats, elk and many edible plants. As a result of this rich environment, these people developed a complex society. The most famous people of the Northwest Coast are the Kwakiutl who are famous for their celebrations known as Potlatches. The Northwest Coast is known for its magnificent wooden carvings, such at totem polls and other works of art that are admired throughout the world. Tribes of the Northwest Coast include the Tlingit, Tsimshian, Haida, Kwakiutl, Nootka, Chinook Salish, Makah, and Tillamook.

THE SUBARCTIC CULTURE AREA

The subarctic region comprises the larger part of Canada and interior Alaska, stretching from the Atlantic to the Pacific oceans. This area begins about 200 miles north of the United States/Canadian border and continues for hundreds of miles. Since the eastern half of this region was once covered by glaciers, the soil is poor and due to the short growing season, agriculture is not possible. As a result the people hunt and fish. In order to follow the food, the people originally had no permanent homes and traveled with the seasons.

White contact brought diseases that killed many people and caused the local cultures to decline. Many of these events took place in living memory. As a result, many people continue to be impacted by these horrible memories.

Although the people now live in villages and are no longer nomadic, many Subarctic Indians continue to trap, fish, hunt commercially, and practice a subsistence way of life that is based on fishing and hunting. These people are admired for their ability to preserve their traditional way of life even when adjusting to modern circumstances.

THE ARCTIC CULTURAL AREA

The Arctic cultural area rings Alaska and northern Canada and stretches into Asia and Greenland. Agriculture is impossible and people live by fishing and by hunting seal, caribou, and, in some places, whales. The arctic, of course, is also the home of the Inuit (commonly known as the Eskimo[1]), a group that is distinct from the other Native people of the region. Like the Subarctic peoples, they retain much of their ancient way of life due to their remote locations.

As was the case with the subarctic peoples, epidemics brought by White contact killed many people. Many of these epidemics took place in recent times and their memory is still hurtful to many living people (Napoleon, 1996).

A COMING TOGETHER

Years ago, I had an opportunity to interview Colonel Tim McCoy, a famous hero of cowboy movies made during the 1930s. At some point in the interview, we began discussing his work with Native American actor Chief Dan George. McCoy observed: "Chief Dan George is a great actor.... He can play a Navaho, an Apache, or an Iroquois all equally well." McCoy realized the big differences between various Native cultures and recognized that somebody who could play an Apache, a Navaho, and an Iroquois was be a great actor, indeed.

Our discussion of various cultural areas also recognizes the tremendous variation between various Native peoples. And these differences, recognized by the people themselves, have often resulted in heated rivalries.

In recent years, members of different Native cultures have begun to focus upon their mutual interests and similar experiences. This is leading to mutually-beneficial cooperation. Some activities are political in nature while others have a cultural orientation (such as Pow Wows that are attended by the members of more then one Native culture or nation). These trends point to a new era of cooperation between different Native peoples.

INTERNAL RIVALRIES

As mentioned above, Native cultures long fought with each other, although this kind of rivalry has largely disappearing today. Nonetheless, tensions often exist among members of the same culture who hold different opinions regarding how to best respond to economic opportunities.

Some Natives (on and off the reservation) place a high value on their traditional culture. In addition, they may embrace a traditional religion and want to preserve a traditional way of life. Others, in contrast, may be more interested in economic opportunity and they may seek to follow a modern lifestyle. Thus, one segment of a particular tribe may oppose gambling and seek to maintain a more traditional lifestyle while their rivals seek to open gambling casinos in order to encourage business and create jobs. Some Alaskan Natives, likewise, may advocate drilling for oil or natural gas while others oppose it. In a similar way, some segments of a Native culture may place a high value of maintaining a subsistence way of life while others consider it to be a doomed and unprogressive throwback to earlier times.

WHAT IS A NATIVE AMERICAN?

As used here, the definition of Native Americans does not rely solely upon blood. Instead, the degree to which a person embraces a Native culture is also considered. As with the Natchez (mentioned above) some Native cultures are extinct even though descendants may continue to live. On the other hand, many people might be only "part Native" biologically, but completely embrace their Native cultural heritage. Thus, even if it might be hard to find a "biologically pure" member of many Native groups, the culture may continue to thrive.

The opposite situation is equally revealing. Some people possess Native blood, but have lost their cultural traditions. Are these people Natives? Genetically, they are, but culturally they are not. The criterion that is used in the United States to establish a Native American identity, furthermore, largely relies upon cultural, not merely genetic considerations. Thus, for a tribe to be recognized, the Native culture and political organization must exist.

This book is primarily concerned with individuals who maintain some sort of cultural identity as Native people. They can do so even if they are also a part of the larger community. While other definitions of "Native" exist, this book focuses on cultural identities and their importance.

COPING WITH SUBSTANCE ABUSE AND CULTURAL IDENTITY

As is widely known, substance abuse is a significant problem among Native people in North America and throughout the world. To a large degree, substance abuse is triggered by the stress and pain people feel. Native substance abusers often complain that the therapy they receive does not address the problems they face as members of the Native community.

Many therapists believe that their Native clients are not serious about recovery because they find fault with the program of recovery offered them. This book takes their complaints at face value. Programs of recovery need to be tailored around the needs of individuals and the vulnerabilities of their cultures.

Indeed, many Native groups are creating programs of recovery that are based upon their unique heritage. Many of these groups make good use of elders and Native methods of communication, such as talking circles. This book is written as one way to channel such powerful cultural forces in a way that can help people recover from substance abuse.

APPENDIX: HAWAIIANS AND MAORI: PARALLEL EXAMPLES

While this book deals primarily with the Natives of North Americans, other Native peoples have been subjected to similar experiences. Two revealing examples are Native Hawaiians and the Maori of New Zealand. By briefly looking at their history, the plight of Native Americans can be better understood and (2) the findings of this book can be applied to other Native peoples from around the world.

HAWAIIANS

Before White contact, the Hawaiian Islands had a population that ranged somewhere between 200,000 (Stannard, 1989) to 800,000 (Bushnell, 1993). They lived in a pleasant world and were well adjusted to it. Just like Native North Americans, the Hawaiian people had no immunity to various European diseases and, as a result, dreadful epidemics followed the first White contact. According to Michael Salzman (2001), the Hawaiians "understood [these epidemics] in the same way that the [Alaskan] Yu'pik understood their great death" (p. 181) and they blamed themselves for the tragedy.

Everybody expected the Native Hawaiian cultures to die off just as the Native American cultures were predicted to quickly and completely disappear (Davis 1968, p. 86.)

Although experiencing hard times for many years, the Hawaiian Native culture is re-emerging as a powerful force. This example is similar to the progress being made by many Native North American cultures. Although North America has its own unique history, their experiences and those of Native Hawaiians are largely parallel.

THE MAORI

The Maori of New Zealand are a Native people who (like Native Hawaiians and Native North Americans) faced trauma as a result of White contact. Comparing the Maori experience to that of Native Alaskans, for example, Gilgen (1996) observes:

There are many similarities between [Native Alaskan and Maori] experiences … a disproportionate over-representation in the prisons, abhorrent statistics regarding disease and health issues, dismal failure in the education system, and the highest ratio of unemployed people in the country. (p. 52)

Gilgen (1996) feels that Native Alaskans are now experiencing what the Maori endured at the turn of the twentieth century. Gilgen continues:

My ancestors were traumatized by a great death, a period in which Maori culture was attacked physically, spiritually, and culturally through disease, land confiscation, inter-tribal warfare, and the introduction of alcohol and non-indigenous religions. To deal with the rape of our land and culture, we also used a range of coping mechanisms that included self-blame, alcohol abuse, violence among ourselves, depression, suicide, and denial. (p. 52)

As in North America, the Native population of New Zealand was reduced to second class citizenship when Whites came to dominate. And these losses often triggered substance abuse: In the areas most affected, the Maoris "were living in debt and confined to run-down reserves, poorly administered because of the confusion of multiple ownership brought about by land courts. Already, South Island Maoris had passed though liquor craze in the mid-1960s which left them " 'squalid, miserable, lifeless' foreshadowing the fate of the North Island tribes later in the decade…. This upturn in drinking assisted in the breakdown in the traditional leadership" (Alcohol Research Unit, 1984, pp. 4-5).

These problems continue:

Alcohol … continues to be a problem today. In 1986, the Maori admission rate for alcohol dependence or abuse was approximately double the non-Maori rate, and I know from my experiences in a Maori community that young people die in alcohol-related accidents and middle aged people die sooner than necessary because of alcohol-related disease. (Harrison, 1996 p. 59)

The examples of Hawaii and New Zealand demonstrate that although the Native people of North America have their own unique histories, their experiences are similar to those of other Native peoples from around the world.

Once Were Warriors: A Dramatic Example

Fiction is often truer than real life. Indeed, a brief review of the feature film *Once Were Warriors* demonstrates how hurtful experiences can transform Native people and result in dysfunctional behavior such as substance abuse. It also shows how cultural rebirth can provide salvation.

The story is about a woman of Maori descent who lives with a violent and wasteful husband who is more concerned with his drinking buddies than with his wife and children.

Jake Heke, the husband has slipped so far into a life of drinking and violence that he is unaware of what a monster he has become. The wife, although strong and vital, is physically weaker than Jake and must bend to his wishes. Not completely broken, she occasionally states her mind, but is bloodied and raped for doing so.

While Jake represents those who cannot break the cycle of oppression, the downtrodden wife shows how people can regain themselves and their heritage. Rebounding from tragedy and misfortune, she embraces the Maori culture and finds freedom, strength, and salvation in doing so.

Two of her sons also regain their heritage and emerge as strong and vital men. One joins a Maori street gang and becomes adorned with traditional Maori tattoos. The other does not alter his body, but internalized the Maori spirit just as much as his brother who accepts outward signs of his identity. Both options are presented as examples of how people can gain strength from their traditions. Native people can return to wholeness by embracing their culture.

Native North Americans as well as other Native peoples have been badly hurt by contact with the outside world. On the one hand, Native people tend to be poor and they are often treated with little respect. Sociologists and psychologists emphasize that the stress caused by such treatment and experiences can trigger dysfunctional behavior, such as alcoholic drinking and substance abuse. Although Native Americans, Hawaiians, and Maori are distinct, their histories and responses have revealing parallels.

NOTES

1. Many people feel the term "Eskimo" is derogatory or at least overly generic and prefer more traditional names for specific people such as Inuit, Inupiaq, and Yup'ik. I use the term because the average person is familiar with it. No disrespect is intended.

REFERENCES

Alcohol Research Unit. (1984). *Alcohol and the Maaori people*. Auckland, New Zealand: Alcohol Research Unit.

Bushnell, O. A. (1993). *The gifts of civilization: Germs and genocide in Hawaii*. Honolulu: University of Hawaii Press.

Davis, G. (1968). *A shoal of time: History of the Hawaiian islands*. Honolulu: University of Hawaii Press.

Gilgen, M. (1996). A response to Harold Napoleon. In H. Napoleon (Ed.), *Yuyaruq: The way of being human*. Fairbanks: Alaska Native Knowledge Network.

Harrison, B. (1996). Response to Yuuyaraq: The way of being human. In H. Napoleon (Ed.), *Yuyaruq: The way of being human*. Fairbanks, AK: Alaska Native Knowledge Network.

Napoleon, H. (1996). *Yuyaruq: The way of being human*. Fairbanks, AK: Alaska Native Knowledge Network.

Salzman, M. (2001). Cultural trauma and recovery: Perspectives from theory management theory. *Trauma, Violence, and Abuse, 2*(2), 172-191.

Stannard, D. E. (1989). *Before the horror*. Honolulu: University of Hawaii Press.

Chapter 3

Why Me?

For generations, it has been observed that Native Americans often suffer from substance abuse. Although other causes exist, this chapter focuses on cultural stress and its impact. By doing so, parallels between Native Americans and other Native people are discussed.

Alcoholism is a puzzling disease. Why do some people become substance abusers while others do not? Nobody knows for sure.

Native alcoholics often ask "Why me?" At first they might have been able to enjoy a few drinks, but for some reason, they lost control. "How can this happen?", many people want to know.

It has long been observed that Native Americans have been particularly hard hit by the alcohol and substance abuse. A number of theories explore this tendency. Some insist that Native people are vulnerable for biological reasons. Others point to cultural causes and the fact that many Native people become substance abusers due to stress and unhappiness. Although biological and cultural theories are very different, on many occasions both factors might be working together. Thus, both biological and social influences might combine to make Natives especially vulnerable to substance abuse, especially alcoholism. Each theory will be discussed separately.

BIOLOGICAL REASONS

The "firewater myth" suggests that Native Americans are particularly vulnerable to alcohol for biological reasons (Mail & Johnson, 1993.)

The belief has been around for many years. Both Benjamin Franklin and members of the Lewis and Clark expedition noticed that, once they start, Native people tend to drink to the point of intoxication and their drinking often led to violence (Duncan &

Duncan, 1995). Such ideas are also found in Zane Grey's famous novel *The Vanishing American* (1927) where the hero is a Native boy who, being adopted by White parents and raised in the East, had little contact with his own people. Even without contact with other Natives, he falls victim to alcoholism. With the support of his lover and by embracing a program of complete abstinence, however, our hero conquers his affliction and reasserts himself as a role model for others to follow. Because Grey wrote before Alcoholics Anonymous was founded, his ideas reflect the beliefs of the 1920s, not the preaching of self help groups that sprung up a few years later. One way of explaining this vulnerability begins by observing that in many parts of the world (such as Europe), people have been drinking alcoholic beverages for thousands of years. As a result, White people evolved in a manner that somewhat protects them from alcohol (even though alcoholism continues to be a problem among those of European descent.)

In the Americas, there was no widespread use of alcoholic beverages until the era of white contact. (The only example of consuming alcoholic beverages of which I am aware is the custom of fermenting the sap of the Sugar Maple tree during the spring in the Northeastern portion of North America. This, however, only produced a mildly alcoholic beverage that was available during a short season of the year, a situation that would prevent frequent drinking that could result in alcoholism.)

Because Native Americans did not drink until fairly recently, the forces of evolution did not worked to reduce their vulnerability to alcohol. As a result, once Native Americans started drinking, these people were especially likely to become alcoholics.

Native people are more susceptible to many diseases than the White people who brought them to America. Although the common cold is merely a minor annoyance among most White people, for example, it killed of large numbers of Native people who had never been exposed to the disease and, as a result, had no resistance to it.

Many people explain the vulnerability of Native people to alcohol in the same way. Because alcohol never existed until the Whites came, Native Americans did not build up a resistance to it. Although popular, researching this theory is difficult (Snipp, 1997) and as Garcia-Andrade, Wall, and Ehlers have observed (1997), there is no evidence that demonstrates that Native Americans have a higher psychological or physiological tendency towards alcoholism than any other group of people. In addition, drinking patterns vary widely among various Native American groups and no one pattern of drinking dominates (Mail & Johnson, 1993). This fact draws the firewater myth into question.

This book, while it does not take sides regarding the firewater myth, looks for additional causes of alcoholism within the Native community.

SOCIAL IMPACTS

Another set of theories links substance abuse among Native Americans to cultural and social causes. Some researchers notice that Native Americans have long used mind altering drugs within a religious setting (Abbott, 1996) or to trigger spiritual experiences (Kahn, 1986; Mail & McDonald, 1980). They then suggest that these experiences might lead to alcoholic drinking. Although these theories are interesting, I sense that there is a difference between a person participating in a structured religions ceremony and passing out drunk in the gutter. Suggesting that religious practices can trigger substance abuse, furthermore, conflicts with the well respected theory that when people use alcohol in a positive and constructive manner, alcoholism declines.

Another chain of thought points out that due to poverty and the prejudices of others, Native people experience a great deal of stress and that these pressures can trigger substance abuse. Writing about ethnic groups in general, Al-Issa (1997) has argued that drinking patterns among various ethnic groups tend to be influenced by:

1. The stress people face when living in an alien environment,
2. Socio-economic stress including being poverty stricken, and
3. The tensions inherent in minority status.

In my mind, these are important causes of substance abuse among Native North Americans, even though a biological vulnerability might exist.

SPECIFIC NEEDS OF NATIVE AMERICANS

Many Native Americans complain that they are not well served by programs of recovery programs that are based on Alcoholics Anonymous because they believe that this program does not deal with their experiences and feelings. Many members of the counseling profession agree that Alcoholics Anonymous often does not help a large percentage of Native people.

The ineffectiveness of Alcoholics Anonymous among Native people may be the result of differences between those who founded Alcoholics Anonymous and Native people who seek to recover from alcoholism. While the founders of Alcoholics Anonymous were White and middle class, Native people come from different cultural traditions and face a variety of pressures that are not addressed by Alcoholics Anonymous. While Alcoholics Anonymous is a valuable program, many Native people feel the need to supplement it with others methods of recovery.

A method of tailoring programs of recovery around the needs of specific people is badly needed. And it must be able to deal with cultural differences and with the social and economic problems that impact Native communities (such as low social status, prejudice, and poverty.)

To make matters worse, many Native Americans, suffer from what can be called "cultural genocide," the process of stripping away a people's heritage even though they continue to live. In some cases this just happens as the world changes. On other occasions, the dominant society has systematically sought to destroy the cultural heritage of Native people. In both cases, the pain of this process can be too much for people to bear. When cultures and societies are quickly destroyed, profound unhappiness and dysfunctional behavior, such as substance abuse, can easily result. Since cultural destruction has long been a fact of live among Native People, we can expect a large number of people to develop patterns of substance abuse as a form of self-medication that deadens the pain people feel.

Many Native programs of recovery actively seek to build recovery around the traditional culture. As Fred Beauvais (1998) has observed:

> Many Indian people believe that the loss of their culture is the primary cause of many of their existing social problems, especially those associated with alcohol. Many of the community-based alcohol treatment programs in Indian communities across the country have strong a cultural or spiritual component that is intended to revitalize traditional beliefs and serve as the primary source of individual strength in maintaining sobriety. (p. 7)

Although Beauvais complains that such ideas are not easily studied in "scientific ways," they are profoundly important. This book provides you with a way of dealing with them.

It is important to clearly recognize the degree to which traditional cultures, such as those of various Native American communities, are under attack by many powerful social and economic forces. We should never forget that Native American cultures have been (and will continue to be) under profound attack and that the stress that results from these assaults takes its toll by, among other things, triggering a vulnerability to substance abuse.

In recent years, members of the counseling profession have been urged to (1) become aware of their own values and biases (2) become aware of the world view of their clients, and (3) choose appropriate strategies of intervention (see Arredondo & McDavis, 1992

pp. 444-446). The basic concern driving this movement is that, on many occasions, clients may not be well served by counseling that does take the cultural dimension into account. People who seek recovery need a clear vision of who they are and the unique needs that they possess. By developing this awareness, Native substance abusers can most effectively pursue programs of recovery.

While people may be a part of their own Native culture, they also tend to be connected with the larger community. As a result, they might have a niche in two different and conflicting worlds. This situation can put people between a rock and a hard place in ways that lead to stress and the dysfunction it can cause. By reducing this stress or by channeling it in positive and productive ways, the vulnerability to substance abuse can be reduced. An important goal of this book is to help Native people cope with substance abuse in this way.

PARTING COMMENTS

Some people believe that Native people have an inborn weakness to become alcoholics. Although this theory has not been proven, many people are convinced that it is true. In addition, Native cultures are often under attack and many Natives live in poverty and suffer a lack the opportunity build a better life. These hurtful situations can trigger substance abuse.

Although substance abuse is a universal problem facing all people, it seems to impact Native people in specific ways. Unfortunately, many strategies of recovery that were created within White society may not be completely appropriate for Native American populations. While existing programs should not be completely discarded, they may need to be supplemented with methods that acknowledge and embrace Native traditions.

One mainstream method that stems from the White experience, is Alcoholics Anonymous/the 12 Step Program. On the one hand, Alcoholics Anonymous was developed by and for the mainstream population, even though it has been adjusted to help many other groups. On the other hand, Alcoholics Anonymous seems to assume that a stable society exists for the alcoholic to return to once they enter a meaningful recovery. As a result, Alcoholics

Anonymous does not deal with profound cultural losses experienced by many Native people. It also does not adequately deal with the social disruption caused by uncontrolled social change. As a result of these limitations, it appears that Alcoholics Anonymous needs to be supplemented with programs that deal with the particular types of losses that Native people so often face.

Clearly, programs that deal Native substance abusers are sorely needed. Many Native alcoholics ask "Why me?" This is not an easy question to answer. There might be biological reasons. And certainly cultural explanations provide valuable clues. In particular, rapid social change and the pain it can cause are likely causes. Hopefully, by keeping these possible influences in mind, you can begin to understand who you are and what causes your pain.

REFERENCES

Abbott, P. J. (1996). American Indian and Alaska Native Aboriginal use of alcohol in the United States. *American Indian and Alaska Native Mental Health Research, 7*(2), 1-13.

Arredondo, D. W., P., & McDavis, R. J. (1992). Multicultural Counseling Competencies and Standards: A Call to the Profession. *Journal of Counseling and Development, 70.*

Beauvais, F. (1998). American Indians and Alcohol. *Alcohol Health and Research World, 22*(4), 253-260.

Garcia-Andrade, C., Wall, T. L., & Ehlers, C. L. (1997). The Firewater Myth and response to alcohol in Mission Indians. *American Journal of Psychiarty, 154,* 983-958.

Grey, Z. (1927). *The Vanishing American.* New York: Grosset & Dunlap.

Kahn, M. (1986). Psychological disorders of Aboriginal people of the United States and Australia. *Journal of Rural Community Psychology, 7,* 45-59.

Mail, P. D., & Johnson, S. (1993). Boozing, sniffing and toking: An overview of past, present, and future of substance use by American Indians. *American Indian and Alaska Mental Health Research, 5*(1). 1-33.

Mail, P. D., & McDonald, D. R. (1980). *Tulapai to Takani: A bibliography of alcohol use and abuse among Native Americans of North America.* New Haven, CT: HRAF Press.

Snipp, M. (1997). Some observations about racial boundaries and the experiences of American Indians. *Ethnic and Racial Studies, 20,* 665-689.

Prologue to Part 2
Cultural Distress and Individual Dysfunction

As was discussed in the first section of this book, people are often badly hurt because their cultures are weakening or because they can no longer relate to their heritage. This can result in pain and sorrow that can trigger substance abuse. Chapters 4 and 5 deal with this reality.

Chapter 4 reminds us that for many years people tended to assume that all substance abusers were pretty much the same because they all had trouble with their drinking and/or drugging. While focusing on similarities is useful in many ways, this approach can also draw our attention away from important differences. Native cultures, for example, often face decline and stress and many Native people have lost

touch with their traditions. The resulting pain and tensions can trigger substance abuse.

Chapter 5 continues this conversation by noting that when cultures are weakened they may become unable to protect their members from the stress and pain that triggers substance abuse. The goal of these chapters is to provide a better foundation for understanding how cultural change and the tensions that it causes might trigger substance abuse. Native people are often negatively affected by these hurtful forces. As a result, although substance abuse is a universal disease, Native people often experience it in special ways.

Chapter 4

Diversity and Recovery

For many years, self help groups and counselors have focused upon how all substance abusers are the same because they all relate to drugs and/or alcohol in dysfunctional ways. Focusing on similarities can cause important differences to be ignored. Due to stress and cultural decline, for example, Native substance abusers often face distinct pressures and pains not experienced by the mainstream population.

It is a fact of life that people start out largely the same, but become very different because of their cultures. While people may have powerful instincts like animals, their culture also exerts a strong influence. Dogs from Germany, China, and the United States may act and think pretty much the same, but people from these countries are very different. These variations can be a source of both strength and pain.

People should use their culture and heritage as tools of recovery. Although this suggestion is completely sensible, therapists and self-help groups often act in an opposite manner and concentrate upon similarities, not distinctiveness.

Alcoholics Anonymous, for example, emphasizes that all alcoholics are the same. People are even warned that if they center upon how they are different recovery may not occur. In the folklore of Alcoholics Anonymous, this is called "defining yourself out of the program," a situation that exists when people come to believe that because they are different in some way they don't need to follow the AA path as prescribed. Many Alcoholics Anonymous members warn that such people are likely to fail. People are told, to remember that they are alcoholics, like millions of other people, and that they should act accordingly. Today we increasingly recognize important differences between people and that these differences contribute both to addiction and recovery.

In order to demonstrate these important changes in our thinking about recovery we will first talk about

Alcoholics Anonymous and how it views all alcoholics as being the same. This will be followed by briefly looking at programs that emphasize differences.

ALCOHOLICS ANONYMOUS

Alcoholics Anonymous (much of this discussion applies to Narcotics Anonymous as well) helps us to understand that being an alcoholic is suffering from a disease. Due to the efforts of Alcoholics Anonymous, the world began to see alcoholics as sick people needing help. This was the first big step forward that has helped millions of people. This perspective, however, makes it easy to envision all alcoholics as similar because they all seem to suffer from the same disease. Planning a program of recovery with this in mind, Alcoholics Anonymous members typically advocate that all alcoholics to use a similar plan or method when they seek recovery. Members, for example, are told to embrace a higher power and use this relationship as the tool that builds toward sobriety. The Alcoholics Anonymous literature goes so far as to depict non-belief in God (or a higher power) as a personality trait that might have triggered alcoholic behavior, in the first place, and might prevent recovery.

Alcoholics Anonymous, of course, recognizes that different people believe in different Gods. As a result, the Alcoholics Anonymous literature uses phrases such as "God, as we understood him" to make the program appropriate for many different people and religions. The particular vision of God/higher power (personal, good, caring, rational, male etc.), closely reflects the Christian God and does not reflect many other religions. Many alcoholics complain that Alcoholics Anonymous seems to embrace religious beliefs even though it tries not to do so.

The cornerstone of Alcoholics Anonymous is the "12 step program" that begins when people admit they are powerless over alcohol. This confession is followed by embracing the notion of the aforementioned "higher power" that, although officially expressed in the most general of terms in the Alcoholics Anonymous literature, closely resembles the Christian God.

Having enlisted the aid of some sort of higher power, individuals are urged to assess their lives, acknowledge their shortcomings (to themselves, God, and another person), and do penance in appropriate ways that do not hurt others. Having gotten one's substance abuse under control with the help of a higher power, a spiritual rebirth is predicted and members are told to "practice these principles in all their affairs."

Another specific emphasis of the Alcoholics Anonymous/12 Step Program is that it tends to depict alcoholics being strong willed and dominant people. Alcoholics Anonymous places a great emphasis upon the premise that alcoholics are usually unable to admit that they are not all-powerful and the program predicts that this inability to acknowledge one's limitations can result in alcoholic drinking.

A lot of what Alcoholics Anonymous has to say is a reflection of its cofounder Bill Wilson, who wrote much of the Alcoholics Anonymous literature. Being a strong-willed individual, Wilson believed his alcoholism was caused by his inability to control the world around him. And believing he was a typical alcoholic, he thought everybody slipped into alcoholism in the same way that he did. As a result, Wilson thought all alcoholics should practice the program of recovery that worked for him.

It seems to me that Wilson believed he was like every other alcoholic. But he was wrong because he had his own personality and other people have theirs. The program he created for himself might not work for you.

Nonetheless, some members of AA stand by Wilson and his teachings. One of the classic catch-phrases from Alcoholics Anonymous, for example, is "terminal uniqueness" which suggests that if people focus on how they are different, they will never be able to benefit from Alcoholics Anonymous and the recovery it has to offer.

Many substance abuse counselors, furthermore, are successful veterans of Alcoholics Anonymous or Narcotics Anonymous. As a result, many treatment options are based on the example of Alcoholics Anonymous/Narcotics Anonymous and the 12 Step Program. Indeed, a basic goal of many residential therapy programs is to prepare participants to join Alcoholics Anonymous or Narcotics Anonymous upon their release.

AA/NA and the 12 Steps, of course, are very valuable tools and I have much praise for them. But some people may be best served by other methods of recovery.

THE IMPORTANCE OF DIFFERENCES

Today, new programs for combating alcoholism and substance abuse are becoming more popular. One is the Secular Organization for Recovery (SOS) that eliminates the religious nature of Alcoholics Anonymous (Christopher, 1992, 1997). Rational Recovery (Trimpey, 1985) and Self Management and Recovery Training (Hovarth, 1997) are based on the rationalistic therapy methods developed by Albert Ellis. Both of them also offer non-spiritual and non-religious programs of recovery for those who suffer from alcoholism.

Other organizations, such as Women for Sobriety (Kirkpatrick, 1978, 1990), seek to help alcoholic women as a group of people having their own needs. Women for Sobriety, for example, argues that women have special needs that revolve around self-esteem and guilt. The program deals with problems facing women while, at the same time, combating substance abuse. In all these cases, new programs of recovery seek to serve specific groups of people. They insist that a specialized program is more effective than general programs, such as Alcoholics Anonymous, that attempt to help all people to recover in exactly the same way.

Cultural differences of course, are very important and can influence both substance abuse and recovery. Hispanic men often embrace a "macho" personality and, as a result, they may have trouble admitting they are powerless over alcohol or anything else. Some Native Americans people are rather private and reserved and, as a result, they may not be comfortable talking in public about their failures (or even their achievements) as Alcoholics Anonymous and the 12 Step Program encourages.

And since Alcoholics Anonymous was created by middle class White men, other people might not respond to it very well. A number of Afro-Americans have told me that they are uncomfortable with Alcoholics Anonymous and have trouble with the program for that reason. I have heard numerous Native Americans in recovery make similar complaints.

Thus, after a long era in which substance abusers were viewed in terms of their similarities, we are in an era in which diversity is viewed as very important. Today we understand that the culture of a substance abuser (among other things) may contribute both to the disease and to recovery.

THINKING ABOUT DIVERSITY

What exactly do we mean by diversity? I will provide a partial explanation by discussing concepts that can be used to distinguish differences. They include (1) Rational versus irrational, (2) Religious versus agnostic, (3) Sex/sexual orientation, and (4) Cultural. This is merely a list that pops into my mind. Perhaps you can think up other terms that are useful to you. In any event, we will briefly discuss each of these concepts.

RATIONAL VERSUS IRRATIONAL

Some individuals are best able to seek recovery by using rational thought. They can recover by attacking their substance abuse in a highly structured and well-thought out manner. These individuals tend to believe that people (1) possess the power of reason and rational thought and (2) recovery can best be gained by using these tools.

An alternative position, in contrast, is to believe that although people might be rational, at the core, people are emotional. The famous psychiatrist, Sigmund Freud, for example, believed that people are largely like animals and respond in emotional ways eve if they do not know this is true. Those who accept this belief will seek strategies of recovery that deal with feelings and emotions, not rational abilities.

RELIGIOUS VERSUS AGNOSTIC

Many people are religious and, in America, the vast majority of people believe in a personal God that has a conscious personality, created the world, and so on. Christians, for example, tend to view God as a the father of mankind, as well as the force that consciously established specific rules that are intended to govern both nature and human behavior. Those holding such beliefs may view recovery as adjusting to God's will.

Other people do not believe in a personal God. They tend to view mankind as part of nature and they emphasize the need for people to fit into the natural order of things. Dealing with recovery in terms of God does not make sense to such people.

SEXES/SEXUAL ORIENTATION

Some people feel that there are very real differences between the sexes and/or people with different sexual orientations. Those who believe that this is true are likely to feel that different programs of recovery from are needed for each sex and for individuals who have different sexual orientations.

Others feel that all people are pretty much the same in spite of sexual differences. These people, however, may recognize that sexual identities and orientations can create problems and pressures for people that might trigger substance abuse. Some people, for example, view their sexual preferences as wrong or shameful. As a result, many gays and lesbians experience profound feelings of guilt and shame regarding their lifestyle and sexual desires. These feelings can trigger a desire to the escape this is provided by substance abuse.

CULTURAL

For a variety of reasons, members of some cultures seem to more vulnerable to substance abuse than others. In addition, certain cultures may be under stress and, therefore, their members may be particularly vulnerable to alcoholism.

Alcoholics Anonymous was created by members of mainstream American culture in the 1930s. Once the program was established, efforts were made to generalize it in order to deal with a wider range of people. But in doing so, profound cultural differences were ignored, in spite of sincere and conscious efforts to adjust the program so it could deal with diversity.

IS THE CULTURE VULNERABLE?

Alcoholics Anonymous was founded by people whose culture was healthy and not under vulnerable to outside forces (even though these alcoholics might have become alienated from their culture due to their drinking.) In many parts of the world, in contrast, Native and traditional cultures are under profound attack and the resulting stress can easily trigger substance abuse. Alcoholics Anonymous/the 12 Step Program, however, did not evolve in ways that conveniently deal with this issue.

Today, more than ever before, there is a recognition that alcoholism is a complex disease that impacts different people in many ways. By the same token, therapy and recovery are equally complicated. Going beyond Alcoholics Anonymous' universal program that seeks to provide the same tools of recovery to all people, a wide variety of options are being tailored around the needs of specific people. Native people and their cultures often need programs of recovery that deal with the particular problems they face. Creating a program that acknowledges the importance of the culture and heritage is consistent with current trends of treatment and recovery that are emerging in other contexts.

This book provides a method for dealing with those who fall into a pattern of substance abuse due to cultural pressures. It does so by providing strategies that are designed to help people embrace their heritage in positive ways. You might benefit from such an approach.

REFERENCES

Christopher, J. (1992). *SOS sobriety: The proven alternative to twelve step programs.* New York: Prometheus Books.

Christopher, J. (1997). *How to stay sober: Sobriety without religion.* New York: Prometheus Books.

Kirpatrick, J. (1978). *Turnabout: Help For a new life.* New York: Doubleday.

Kirkpatrick J. (1990). *Stages of a new life program.* New York: Doubleday.

Trimpey, J. (1985). *Rational recovery: The new cure for substance addiction.* New York: Pocket Books.

Chapter 5

Stress and Dysfunction

Stress, fear, and sadness (and other hardships) can trigger substance abuse. Concepts such as the "empty self" and "terror management" provide useful and easily understood ideas of how this takes place.

THE "EMPTY SELF" AND SUBSTANCE ABUSE

The concept of the "empty self "begins with the observation that today's world tends to be "sorely lacking in community and tradition" (Cushman, 1990, p. 607) and that people are disconnected from each other, unfulfilled, and unhappy. Miller (1998) notes that this "theory can be readily applied in addiction counseling by assisting the client in developing a recovery lifestyle that includes a sense of family, community, and tradition, all supportive of the addiction recovery" (p. 17).

The concept of the empty self emphasizes that people are leaving the countryside and moving to town. Many people are less religious than they were in the past. Industrialization is replacing the old ways. These changes are breaking down families, cultures, and communities. As a result, many people have difficulty dealing with others in fruitful and fulfilling ways.

Talking about America, in general, Cushman (1990) complains people are too individualistic. He says:

> I think the vast majority of White middle-class Americans are suffering precisely because they are so individualistic they can't cooperate, participate in group action and sacrifice individual gain for group goals. These are all qualities of self that people must possess

in order to be members of a cohesive community. (p. 543).

I personally feel that Cushman's (1990) emphasis upon individualism causes him to ignore other hurtful forces. Many Native people, for example, may not be particularly individualistic but they have become disoriented and vulnerable because their culture is rapidly changing and is under attack. Thus, more is going on than merely some sort of unhealthy individualism. Nonetheless, the concept of the empty self usefully draws attention to how uncontrolled cultural change can trigger dysfunction and substance abuse.

LOOKING AT SOCIETY

Although the idea of the empty self comes from psychology, it parallels important social theories. The concept of anomie describes a world that has been turned upside down by rapid change. Sociologist, Robert Merton (1957), describes situations where people can no longer achieve their goals in socially acceptable ways. If these people remain loyal to their traditions, they find themselves locked into a battle they cannot win. As a result, people often retreat from the world. Substance abuse is one form of retreat. As with the concept of the empty self, anomie provides a way of understanding how the breakdown of culture or society can cause pain that triggers dysfunctional behavior such as substance abuse.

A SIMILAR VIEW FROM ANTHROPOLOGY

Many Native people are familiar with anthropology because so many anthropologists study Native people. Besides merely studying other people, Anthropologists often help Native communities deal with the problems they face. Anthropologists often reject the popular belief that the Native way of life must fade as modern "civilization" replaces it. David Maybury-Lewis (1977), dismissing that idea, observes: "There is no natural or historic law that militates against small societies. There are only political choices" (pp. 56-61).

Even when change is inevitable, applied anthropologists seek to help Native people to preserve their dignity and their way of life. On many occasions, this can be accomplished by preserving and strengthening the Native culture. Thus, G. N. Appell (1977) insists that "A society undergoing change ... has a right to access to its cultural traditions, its language and its social history" (p. 14).

If the culture is weakened, Appell (1977) complains, people can suffer from what he calls the "social separation syndrome ... [that] involves role conflict and ambiguity, threat to one's self esteem, and an impaired social identity" (p. 14). He continues:

> Social bereavement arising from social change seems to follow a developmental sequence similar to personal bereavement.... There is first a period of denial as numbness accompanied by anxiety, fear, and feelings of threat to one's identity. This is succeeded by a phase of frustrated searching for the lost world or individual, hoping for a reversal and then bitter pining and unrelieved sense of pain.... Following this is a period of depression and apathy.... Finally there is the phase of reorganization when the bereaved begins to build new plans and assumptions about the world. (p. 14)

Note how this idea closely resembles the theories from psychology and the social sciences we discussed earlier. All emphasize that stress and dysfunction can develop when people are cut off from their culture,

traditions and heritage. Breaking the cycle of cultural decline and alienation can help people to overcome their problems.

TERROR MANAGEMENT THEORY: A UNIFYING CONCEPT

Different and conflicting theories are used to explain substance abuse. Terror management theory provides a way to usefully combine these diverse ideas. It emphasizes that people realize that they are going to die and that this knowledge causes fear that can trigger dysfunction. Because they know they will not personally live forever, people often seek to be a part of something that is bigger and more immortal than they are. On many occasions, that bigger and more permanent something is their culture or society. By embracing their culture, they become part of something that will live on after they die. This can be comforting.

When the society is strong and is not in danger of being destroyed, this situation might work just fine. Many Native cultures, however, are so weakened or vulnerable that people no longer believe they will survive. Such pessimistic thoughts can keep people from being comforted by their heritage and lead to stress, pain, and sadness that can trigger dysfunctional behavior, such as substance abuse.

Michael Salzman (2001) has done pioneering work in this area. He argues that when cultures break down people will become increasingly anxious and unhappy. These painful feelings make them vulnerable to substance abuse.

SOME FINAL THOUGHTS

Many Native people have lost touch with their heritage and/or they no longer believe their culture will survive. When people are cut adrift in this way, they can easily become vulnerable to escapist behaviors, such as substance abuse. When everything people hold dear is being destroyed and when their cultures no longer provide safety and guidance, they can easily become dysfunctional.

To a large extent, substance abuse among Native Americans is the result of uncontrolled social change that results in the weakening of traditional cultures.

Since this is true, strengthening Native cultures and embracing their heritage can help Native substance abusers to recover.

RFERENCES

Appell, G. N. (1977). The plight of Indigenous people: Issues and dilemmas. *Survival International Review.*

Cushman, P. (1990). Why the self is empty: Towards a historically situated psychology. *American Psychologist, 45,* 599-611.

Maybury-Lewis, D. (1977). Societies On The Brink. *Harvard Magazine, 1 &2,* 56-61).

Merton, R. (1957). *Social theory and social structure.* New York: The Free Press.

Salzman, M. B. (2001). Cultural Trauma and Recovery: Perspectives From Terror Management Theory. *Trauma, Violence, and Abuse, 2*(2), 172-191.

Prologue to Part 3
The Legacy of Handsome Lake

As our conversation has progressed, we have seen how people can be hurt when their cultures decline or when they lose the ability to respond to their heritage in positive ways. This was followed by discussions of how such hurtful experiences can lead to substance abuse.

A program that helps Native people deal with their heritage in positive ways is suggested by Handsome Lake, an alcoholic Iroquois whose culture was breaking down about 200 years ago. Near death, he returned to sobriety and dedicated himself to cultural renewal and developing a method for helping his people to recovery from substance abuse. His story is retold because of the value of his approach.

In Chapter 6, we will consider the history of the Iroquois people from their days as a strong and vital nation to their "bottom" when they emerged as a beaten people whose continued existence was in significant doubt. During their period of decline, many Iroquois slipped in to alcoholism. Their plight is similar to many Native people today.

Chapter 6

The Terror Facing the Iroquois

The case of the eighteenth century Iroquois is an example of how the decline of a Native culture can lead to anguish that can trigger substance abuse. Hopefully, by looking at the problems that the Iroquois faced long ago, we can understand the challenges that many Native people face today

As we have discussed, many Native American people suffer because their cultures are under severe attack and are breaking down. When this happens, society can no longer help people cope with the problems of their lives. This situation can result in unhappiness, pain, and suffering. Such feelings can trigger dysfunctional behavior, such as substance abuse.

Instead of just spouting theories, I think it is a good idea to look at some real events and use them to better understand how cultural decline can prevent people from making healthy choices. The example of the Iroquois of New York State (in the late eighteenth and early nineteenth centuries) provides an excellent example. And as we will see in later chapters, it also shows how Native people can rebuild a weakened culture and return it to wholeness.

THE PLIGHT OF THE IROQUOIS

The Iroquois is a good example of the fate of Native cultures that are racked by change caused by the intrusions of the outside world. In the late eighteenth/ early nineteenth centuries, the Iroquois faced severe hardships. As their situation grew worse, more and more Iroquois suffered from dysfunctional behavior, such as substance abuse. The response of the Iroquois, while unique to them in some ways, is tragically similar to the plight of many Native people today.

The Iroquois are (and long have been) an impressive people and a proud nation. Without the aid of "civilized" Europeans, the Iroquois formed a complex structure of government that possessed great sophistication and flexibility. Some observers believe that documents like the United States Declaration of Independence and its Constitution are influenced by the examples provided by the Iroquois government. Everyone agrees that even long ago, the Iroquois were a complicated nation that possessed complex political and social skills. The fact that this people eventually suffered "hard times" does erase the significance of their achievement.

During colonial times, the Iroquois created a nice situation for themselves. They largely conquered their neighbors. Women were farmers and performed various domestic chores. The men were hunters and warriors, ready to protect the society when necessary. In those days, farming was considered to be an unmanly activity.

For many years, the British and the French fought among themselves for control of what is now Quebec and Ontario, Canada and the "Upstate" New York region of the United States. The clever Iroquois were able to play the French against the British and they grew rich in the process. Once the French had been totally defeated, however, the British no longer needed to extend favors to the Iroquois in order to maintain a military allegiance. As a result, hard times began. Thus, in the years before the American War of Revolution, the Iroquois had begun to suffer significant setbacks for the first time in their history.

When the American Revolution began, the Iroquois once again became part of a conflict that was bigger than they were. As had been the case in colonial times, the Iroquois found themselves, caught between rival forces and they had to decide who they would support. Historically, the Iroquois had been allies of the British. From a more practical perspective, most Iroquois realized that the British merely wanted trading partners in America while many settlers from the colonies would probably want to move to Iroquois territory if they won the war. As a result of these fears, most Iroquois fought on the British side.[1]

Although the decision to ally themselves with the British was sensible enough, doing so proved to be costly:

> [During the war, the Iroquois homeland] was devastated by the John Sullivan [United State military commander] expedition in 1778, which in a three pronged offensive managed to burn the houses and the crops in almost every major Iroquois town. Many of the women and children, and the surviving warriors, took refuge at Fort Niagara with the British, who housed them in a refugee camp. They were, inadequately clothed, inadequately fed, inadequately sheltered, and swept by disease. By the end of the war the Iroquois population had been cut approximately in half. (Wallace, 1970, p. 443)

After the war the plight of the Iroquois became increasingly grim. The victorious United States, remembering that many Iroquois had been their enemies in the battle for independence, showed the Iroquois few favors. And, as the Iroquois leaders had predicted, hordes of White settlers were lured to the area. By the turn of the late eighteenth /early nineteenth centuries, the Iroquois were a beaten people who had recently seen their communities destroyed, had been defeated in war and killed off by disease. To make matters worse, the survivors were increasingly besieged by outsiders. As is often the case in such situations, many Iroquois developed dysfunctional ways of life such as alcoholism.

These events, although specific to the Iroquois people, are paralleled by many other Native people, including Native Hawaiians and the Maori of New Zealand. As a result, the story of the Iroquois provides a good example of how stress caused by change, contact, and conflict can hurt people who are unprepared to cope with the circumstances that they must face.

THE TERROR OF DECLINE

Although the history of the Iroquois can stand alone and be understood without the use of any particular theory, the ideas of terror management, discussed in the last chapter provide useful insights. As you may remember, terror management can help us to understand why people cling to their cultures and to their way of life. Although people know they will die, they hope that part of them will live on after they are gone. Since people know they won't live forever, they seek to strengthen and be a part of their culture because they believe it will live on. Because people anticipate their culture will exist forever, it provides security from the fear of their personal death.

The culture, however, can only comfort people as long they believe it is immortal. If people do not believe the culture will survive, it will no longer provide this kind of comfort.

A BROADER VIEW

By focusing upon the fear of death, terror management argues that by being part of a culture that is bigger than they are, people can live on after death. In a very real way, for example, George Washington never died because the country he helped create still exists. By serving their culture and being part of it, people can become immortal. But is this all that is going on? Isn't it equally possible for people to support their culture because they believe that doing so is right and proper? Isn't it possible for people to want their culture (or society, or profession, or family, etc.) to survive because they love it? Of course this is possible.

Expanding terror management to deal with such situations is easy. While some people might seek some kind of immortality, others may be motivated for other reasons. The same person, of course, may embrace and support their culture for multiple reasons.

THE IROQUOIS AND TERROR MANAGEMENT

For many generations before the American Revolution, the Iroquois had been a strong and vital people. Under these conditions, the Iroquois were able to live according to their traditions.

The first major blow to the Iroquois position came after the end of the French and Indian War. Once the French surrendered, all of Northeast North American came under British control and these victors no longer needed to lavish favors and trade goods on the Iroquois. While the British did not attack the Iroquois, the support of the British dried up. This situation created hardships for the Iroquois. But the worst was yet to come.

During the American Revolution, most Iroquois fought with the British and they were punished for doing so. Villages were burned and as many Iroquois were subjected to a refugee status. The death of a large percentage of the population also took a toll.

After the war, the conditions faced by the Iroquois continued to get worse. White immigrants flooded into traditional Iroquois territory and most of these newcomers practiced modern farming methods. The Iroquois style of agriculture, performed exclusively by women, could not compete against European farming methods and, as a result, the Iroquois began to fall behind economically. Men, however, did not take up farming because they felt it was an unmanly profession. Men preferred to be warriors and hunters, but game became scarce and there were no wars to fight. As a result, many men could not adjust and sank into alcoholism.

If these challenges were not painful enough, diseases and epidemics swept through Iroquois territory killing many members of Iroquois society.

The result of this tragic situation was dysfunctional behavior that included infighting among the Iroquois, personal resignation/depression, various pathological behaviors, and rampant substance abuse.

Many Iroquois began uncontrolled weeping and pining. People began to fear each other (as evidenced by accusations of witchcraft.) Society was breaking down. Psychological depression was commonplace and Wallace (1970) observes that when people were sober, they were likely to be suicidal (pp. 196-201).

It is obvious that Iroquois culture was no longer able to provide comfort to its people. According to terror management (as discussed above), people cling to their culture because it gives them a feeling of immortality and because they love it. But when the culture faces threats that it cannot combat, people lose faith in the culture and its ability to survive. Placed in such an unenviable situation, many Iroquois could not deal with the pain they faced

BEYOND THE IROQUOIS

Although the Iroquois are a distinct people, the pain they faced so long ago is similar to what many Native peoples today. Disease, economic decline, and cultural decay often occur when Native people confront the outside world. Although the history of the Iroquois is theirs alone, their situation may remind you of what your own people face. If this is true, the Iroquois example may have something important to say to you.

NOTE

1. As a nation, the Iroquois did not have a pro-British policy; instead individual groups were allowed to make their own decision regarding the war. Most, however, sided with the British.

REFERENCE

Wallace, A. F. C. (1970). *The death and rebirth of the Seneca*. New York: Vintage Books.

Chapter 7

Handsome Lake
Hero of the Iroquois

Just when Iroquois culture was at its lowest ebb and its survival was in doubt, Handsome Lake, a long suffering alcoholic, staged a remarkable recovery. More than that, he devised a way for others to recover from substance abuse and for his culture to stop its decline. According to Handsome Lake, for a culture to survive, it needs healthy members. For people to be healthy, furthermore, the culture needs to be strong and vital.

In the late 1700s, Handsome Lake was an alcoholic who seems to be at the end of his productive life. He, like many other Iroquois of his day, had become an alcoholic because changing times had destroyed his world.

At the last possible moment, Handsome Lake stopped drinking, became a powerful leader, and brought the Iroquois back from near extinction. As a result of his efforts, the Iroquois continue to be a proud people even today.

Handsome Lake's recipe for stemming the tide of social and personal decay includes cultural rebirth coupled a personal recovery and penance for past misdeeds. By championing both cultural renewal and personal recovery and by pointing to a strong relationship between the two, Handsome Lake stemmed the tide of despair and hopelessness so widespread among the Iroquois.

Handsome Lake lived during a time of pain and sorrow. Due to White contact, his people went from being proud and free to beaten and hopeless. Handsome Lake, however, helped the Iroquois find new strength. As a result, people regained faith in their culture and came to believe it would survive. This, in turn, helped reverse the sadness and anxiety that had been triggering dysfunctional behavior, such as substance abuse.

Although Handsome Lake directed his efforts towards his own people (the Iroquois), the lessons he taught can be useful embraced by other Native peoples. As a result, Handsome Lake's example and his teachings can be used as the foundation for a program by which other Native people can recover from substance abuse. In this chapter, Handsome Lake and his legacy of cultural rebirth and recovery are presented as an inspirational story of cultural and personal rebirth. In order to show this is not just an isolated example, Handsome Lake and his work will be compared to the writings and suggestions of Harold Napoleon, a modern Native American who suggests a similar course of action.

THE DECLINE OF THE IROQUOIS

As stated above, the life of Handsome Lake is a story of a return to personal sobriety coupled with a cultural rebirth that makes recovery possible. By examining these two different aspects of his life and work, it becomes possible to better understand substance abuse among Native American people and, how it can be overcome.

The story starts during an era of defeat, disease, economic hardship. The Iroquois found themselves unable to cope with the situations they faced. This kind of situation has often been seen among other Native people who face powerful outside forces. When powerful outside forces exert hurtful pressures, dysfunctional behavior and substance abuse often occur.

The Iroquois faced a seemingly hopeless situation. The failure of the old ways triggered widespread sorrow which led, in turn, to dysfunctional "escapist" behavior, including widespread alcoholism. These events, created a vicious circle; people, already demoralized and dysfunctional, sunk lower and lower as conditions grew increasingly worse. Under these conditions, the survival of Iroquois culture was in serious question.

The situation of the Iroquois is hardly unique. A recent and particularly well respected analysis of a similar response is provided by Harold Napoleon, a contemporary Yup'ik Eskimo who, like Handsome Lake, is a recovering alcoholic. And like Handsome Lake, Harold Napoleon (1996) clearly links the decline of his people (and the resulting tendencies towards alcoholism) to the impacts of White contact. He observes:

> When the first White men arrived ... the people did not immediately abandon their old ways. It is an historical fact that they resisted Russian efforts to colonize them.... They were not impressed by the White men, even though they quickly adopted their technology and goods. (p. 9)

Like the situation of the Iroquois many years before, after a period when his people were able to compete and maintain their culture, White contact eventually lead to a horrible crisis caused by disease. Napoleon (1996) tells us:

> The changes were brought about as a result of the introductions of diseases that had been born in the slums of Europe during the dark and middle ages, diseases carried by the traders, the whalers, and the missionaries. To these diseases, the Yup'ik and other Native tribes had no immunity and ... they would lose up to 60% of their people. As a result of epidemics, the Yup'ik world would go upside down; it would end. (pp. 9-10)

These epidemics, which occurred from time to time, culminated in the "Great Death" of 1900. "Out of the suffering, confusion, desperation, heartbreak, and trauma was born a new generation of Yup'ik people. They were born into shock. They woke to a world in shambles, many of their beliefs strewn around them, dead" (Napoleon, 1996, p. 11).

Napoleon (1996) describes this situation in ways that closely resembles the various theories we looked at earlier:

> The world the survivors woke to was without anchor. The *andalkug* [medicine men], their medicines, and their beliefs had all passed away overnight. They woke up to shock, listless, confused, bewildered, heartbroken, and afraid. Like soldiers on an especially gruesome battlefield, they were shell shocked.... Famine, starvation and disease resulting from the epidemic continued to plague them through the 1950s and many more perished. These were the people whom the missionaries would call wretched, lazy, even listless. Gone were the people who Nelson so admired. The long night of suffering had begun for the survivors of the Great Death and their descendants. (pp. 12-13)

Thus, the demoralized situation that Handsome Lake faced in the late eighteenth and early nineteenth is clearly similar to what Napoleon (1996) describes. Both the Iroquois and the Yup'ik were completely unable to deal with the trauma they faced.

STRESS AND DYSFUNCTION

The Iroquois of the late eighteenth century had clearly lost their cultural balance and their spiritual grounding. Here were people facing terrible obstacles that required thoughtful, reasoned, and sober solutions to the problems they faced. But their behavior was the total opposite of what was needed. This horrible situation resulted in further cultural decay/decline and even more dysfunctional behavior.

The hurtful experiences that the Iroquois endured triggered widespread alcoholism. Once these dysfunctions took hold, furthermore, they developed a momentum of their own, further destroying both the Iroquois nation and its individual members.

The Yup'ik suffered in a similar way, although their decline was triggered primarily by disease. Even when people's lives seemed to be improving, the suffering continued. According to Napoleon (1996):

> As their physical lives have improved, the quality of their lives has deteriorated.... Since the 1960s there has been a dramatic rise in alcohol abuse, alcoholism, and associated violent behaviors, which have upset family and village life and resulted in physical and psychological injury, death, and imprisonment. Something self-destructive, violent, frustrated, and angry had been set loose from within Alaska Native people. And it is the young that are dying, going to prison, and maiming themselves. Their families, their friends, their villages say they cannot understand why. Every suicide leaves a stunned family and village. Every violent crime and every alcohol related death elicits the same reaction. The alcohol-related nightmare has now become an epidemic. (pp. 21-22)

This dysfunction behavior was caused by spiritual pain not by physical needs. "One thing we do know-the primary cause of the epidemic is not physical depravation. Native people have never had it so good in terms of food, clothing, and shelter" (Napoleon, 1996, p. 22).

The basic point is that the Yup'ik, as discussed by Napoleon, experienced a pattern of cultural and spiritual decline that almost completely duplicates the situation experienced by Handsome Lake and the Iroquois 200 years earlier. Apparently, profound cultural stress can lead to a breakdown of society that can leave people vulnerable to a wide range of dysfunctional behaviors, such as substance abuse. This is true even if people's physical needs are well taken care of. Although Handsome Lake and Harold Napoleon lived ages apart and 5,000 miles away, they are in almost total agreement regarding substance abuse and its causes.

POSTTRAUMATIC STRESS DISORDER?

Writing in an era when we have seen many Vietnam veterans (many of whom are substance abusers) suffer from posttraumatic stress disorder, Napoleon (1996) uses this disease as a way of describing the pain his people face. According to Napoleon, posttraumatic stress disorder caused by the Great Death triggered the dysfunctional responses of the Yup'ik. Not merely is this theory useful when describing the behavior of the contemporary Yup'ik, it also explains the dysfunctional behavior of the Iroquois during the late eighteenth and and early nineteenth centuries.

The idea of posttraumatic stress disorder is very useful because most people in our culture are familiar with it. This makes the theory particularly helpful when explaining how substance abuse may have become a problem in Native societies and specific members of Native communities.

A DRUNK NAMED HANDSOME LAKE

Within the environment of defeat and despair that the Iroquois faced in the late eighteenth century, Handsome Lake, a once respected member of Iroquois society, had become a pitiful alcoholic. Out of control from drinking and nearly dead, it appeared that his productive life was over. By the spring of 1799, his drinking and its negative impacts had grown steadily worse: "Handsome Lake ... was bedridden, reputedly ... as a consequence of prolonged alcoholic [drinking]" (Wallace, 1978, p. 445).

In the June of that year,

> Handsome Lake collapsed ... in the presence of his daughter; ... he appeared to have died, but actually he was in a trance state and was experiencing the first of a series of visions in which messengers of the Creator instructed him in his own and his people's religious obligations. (Wallace, 1978, p. 445)

After his recuperation from apparent death, Handsome Lake emerged as a new man who dedicated himself to his own sobriety and to the cultural rebirth of Iroquois society.

Eventually Handsome Lake's visions and insights were transformed into a new religion that advocated a new way of life for the Iroquois that could reverse their cultural decline.

On the one hand, Handsome Lake encouraged his people to honor and embrace their cultural traditions.

He warned, however, that they should not merely cling to the past. Handsome Lake encouraged the Iroquois to keep up with the times because the skills of the past were of little value in the new world that was emerging. To make matters worse, acting according to the old ways could condemn the Iroquois to extinction. Iroquois men, for example, refused to farm and as a result, poverty was growing. Men wanted to hunt and be warriors, but they could not do so. White people settling in Iroquois territory brought new methods of agriculture (that included men performing their share of the work) that were more productive than Iroquois women working alone.

Under these trying circumstances, Handsome Lake encouraged Iroquois men to take up farming, urging them to view it as an appropriate vocation that should not trigger shame or embarrassment. Handsome Lake's half brother and collaborator, for example, came to be known as "Cornplanter," a name that underscored that men, as well as women, should farm.

Handsome Lake recognized that the times were changing and the Iroquois people had to adjust. If men farmed, the Iroquois would be in a better position to survive. While pointing to and preserving many Iroquois traditions, he advocated changed that that provided hope and material wellbeing. As a result, society was strengthened and dysfunctional behavior, such as substance abuse, declined.

Handsome Lake also insisted that people cease, on an individual basis, to act in hurtful and dysfunctional ways. Drinking alcoholic beverages was high on the list of banned behaviors.[1] Being an alcoholic himself, Handsome Lake was quite aware of the dangers of alcohol and he strongly discouraged the use of alcoholic beverages.

Handsome Lake also insisted that people acknowledge the sins they had committed and refrain from future misdeeds. Largely through the personal example and the message of Handsome Lake, the Iroquois re-emerged as a vital culture and people. And many Iroquois individuals who had suffered from substance abuse reclaimed their lives through spiritual growth coupled with abstinence. This, in a nutshell, is the history of the heritage and legacy of Handsome Lake. His story is recorded in various places[2] and you are encouraged to read fuller accounts if you are interested. Handsome Lake is a man who having suffered through his own alcoholism, recovered and helped his people to preserve their culture. He and the Iroquois provide one of the great success stories in history.

SIMILAR PRESSURES, SIMILAR SOLUTIONS

As we have discussed, although separated by 200 years and thousands of miles, the experience of Handsome Lake and the Iroquois and Harold Napoleon (1996) and the Yup'ik are almost identical.

Like Handsome Lake, Harold Napoleon (1996) seeks to rebuild the culture by preserving the culture by updating it to suit the times. Both believe that doing so will provide people with the tools they need for recovery.

Napoleon (1996) suggests that if hurtful experiences are not dealt with they will continue to hurt people. He suggests,

> We … have to spend some time just talking to … [the elders]. We would have them truthfully tell their life stories, leaving nothing out. The very oldest are the most important because they will be able to tell their remembrances of the whole village…. They must tell why they gave everything up, why they discarded the old ways, the old beliefs, why they allowed the culture to die…. They are the ones who felt the full brunt of the fatal wounding of their world. (p. 26)

Napoleon (1996) also emphasizes that after the elders have told their story, all members of society need to bare their souls and begin to understand the hurts they have had to endure. He says,

> We must do this because we don't know each other anymore; we have become like strangers to each other. The old do not know or understand the young, and the young do not know or understand the old. Parents do not know their children, and the children do not know their parents. As a result … a gulf has grown between those who love and care for each other the most. (p. 26)

And paralleling Handsome Lake, Napoleon, also encourages Native people to preserve their cultures by transforming them in positive ways that meet the challenges of the future. He recommends,

> It is time to bury the old culture, mourn those who died with it, mourn those who survived it. It is time we buried our many dead who have died in this long night of our suffering, then go forward, lost no more. We have been wandering in a daze for the last 100 years, rocked by a succession of traumatic changes and inundations. Now we have to stop, look at ourselves, and … .press on … free of the past that haunted and disabled us, free of the ghosts that haunted our hearts, free to become what we were intended to be. (pp. 27-28)

Note how both Handsome Lake and Harold Napoleon's (1996) recommend that people who have been battered by circumstance need to transform their lives in positive ways. More then merely getting their personal lives in order, many of the old ways needed to be rethought so they can help people meet the challenges of the future.

At the same time, however, the cultural heritage and its traditions needed to be preserved and embraced. By both preserving the culture while updating it in productive ways, people can more effectively deal with the challenges and pain they face.

CONCLUSION

Handsome Lake, responding to the hurtful events of 200 years ago, created a method cultural renewal that helped his people deal with the pain of cultural decline. By following his instructions, people were better cope with their own dysfunctions. Largely through the efforts of Handsome Lake, the Iroquois people were able to both rebuild their culture and get their personal lives in order. The three steps in Handsome Lake's approach include (1) a re-embrace of the people's cultural traditions, (2) an adjustment of the culture so that it can successfully cope with modern times and (3) overcoming dysfunctional patterns of behavior (such as substance abuse) coupled with a penance for past misdeeds.

The achievements of Handsome Lake are not merely some footnote of years gone by. His ideas are very similar to those of other Native people, such as Harold Napoleon (1996) who seek to preserve and rebuild their culture as they struggle to overcome substance abuse.

The fact that Handsome was a recovering alcoholic, who encouraged people to overcome their substance abuse while atoning for past misdeeds, makes his message even more powerful. And since he urged a cultural renewal that provided the culture with the ability to cope and compete, Handsome Lake suggests tools that link recovery with positive social change that preserves the culture instead of destroying it.

NOTES

1. Others include promiscuous sexual behavior and the practice of witchcraft that was also disruptive to society and (according to Iroquois beliefs) injurious to specific people.

2. Important primary sources include A. F. C. Wallace (editor) "Halliday Jackson's Journal to the Seneca Indians," Thomas S. Abler (editor) *Chainbreaker: The Revolutionary War Memoirs of Govern Blacksnake*, and Arthur C. Parker (editor) *The Code of Handsome Lake*. The most extensive (and respected) secondary work is A. F. C. Wallace's *The Death and Rebirth of the Seneca*. William Fenton and Elisabeth Tooker's "On the Development of the Handsome Lake Religion" is also insightful. It should be noted that there is an extensive researdh tradition on Handsome Lake and this is only a suggestive sampling. For those in the counseling profession, however, it is probably adequate.

REFERENCES

Gilgen, M. (1996). A response to Harold Napoleon's Paper. In H. Napoleon (Ed.), *Yunarag: The way of being human.* Fairbanks, AK: Alaska Native Knowledge Network.

Harrison, B. (1996). Response to "Yuuyaraq." In H. Napoleon (Ed.), *Yunarag: The Way of Being Human.* Fairbanks, AK: Alaska Native Knowledge Network.

Napoleon, H. (1996). *Yunarag: The way of being human.* Fairbanks, AK: Alaska Native Knowledge Network.

Chapter 8

A Path Towards Your Recovery

Handsome Lake suggests a program of recovery that combines cultural well-being with individual recovery. He believed that while the culture should be cherished and protected, it often needs to adjust to the times. Although it is concerned with cultural issues, the Path of Handsome Lake is not at odds with other therapy and self help groups, such as Alcoholics Anonymous. It can be used independently or with other programs of recovery.

As we have seen, Handsome Lake was an Iroquois leader who fell into seemingly incurable alcoholism just when his people were experiencing a terrible decline. After a remarkable recovery, he emerged as the leader who helped his people and their culture to return to health. Many Native cultures and individuals can benefit from this example.

In this discussion, we will talk about Handsome Lake's achievement and show how it can point the way to recovery. This program that reflects his vision will be called "The Path of Handsome Lake."

THE PATH OF HANDSOME LAKE

The Path is a six step program that combines cultural health with individual well-being. The six components suggested by the "Path of Handsome Lake" that are discussed here include (1) Embrace tradition, (2) Transform your traditions and keep them strong, (3) Stop substance abuse and Cultural Apathy, (4) Admit to errors made, (5) Do not repeat errors of the past, and (6) Heritage and recovery are linked.

This course of action (like Alcoholics Anonymous' 12 Step Program) provides a method that constantly reminds people to work towards sobriety. It goes beyond the 12 Step Program, however, because it

deals with the cultural heritage. Before discussing the Path in an overall way, let's first look at each step.

1. **Embrace tradition: "I possess a culture and a tradition. Embracing them is sacred, meaningful, and joyful."**

   As we have discussed, changes forced from the outside world attack and weaken many Native cultures. In addition, many Native people have been forced to abandon their heritage. During the boarding school era in the United States, for example, the educational system serving Native students often made strong efforts to strip Native people of their cultural heritage. Athabascan, Luke Titus of Minto Alaska, for example, told me that when he arrived at boarding school as a young boy he was forced to watch all his Native clothes and possessions being burned. Children in boarding schools often had their mouth washed with soap if they spoke their Native language. Every effort was made to destroy the Native culture in students and make them as much like White people as possible.

   Disease, changing times, and poverty also took their tolls. As a result, many Natives cultures and individuals suffered terribly as a result of contact with the outside world.

Due to this history of contact, traditional cultures have often become weakened. In addition, many Native people have become uncomfortable with their heritage and/or do not know very much about it. When the culture is severely weakened or when people are distanced from it, it can no longer provide the comfort that it once did. Thus, when their cultures break down, Native people may be denied the tools they need to combat dysfunctional behavior, such as substance abuse.

Native people need to understand that they possess a positive cultural heritage that has strength and the power to provide a meaningful and joyous life. But, as we have observed, many Native people know little about their heritage or are separated from it for some reason. Many others have been taught to be embarrassed by their traditions.

Overcoming these obstacles can be very important. It is the first step in the Path of Handsome Lake.

2. **Transform your tradition to keep it strong: "All cultural traditions change and all cultural traditions are under attack. I will strive to help my culture evolve and flourish."**

As we have seen, Native cultures are often under attack and many of the old ways may not work in the modern world. That was true in Handsome Lake's era. By adjusting Iroquois culture, however, Handsome Lake helped the Iroquois people to be successful and Iroquois culture was saved from extinction. As the culture rebounded, dysfunctional behavior such as substance abuse decreased.

Native people experiencing massive social and economic change need to preserve their culture. In many cases, the culture must be adjusted in order to survive. Strong and well-functioning cultures provide comfort to people and relief from the anxieties of life. In order to remain strong and vital, however, cultures often need to be adjusted to changing times and circumstances. All vital cultures go through this process of constant renewal.

In the last hundred years, for example, mainstream American culture has been transformed by the automobile, radio and TV, computers, urbanization, etc. If people struggled to live the way they did at the turn of the twentieth century, life would be traumatic and full of anxiety. But the culture continues to adjust

itself in ways that help people cope. Many people regret some of these changes. Nevertheless, the mainstream culture serves many people reasonable well and helps many people deal with the anxieties and problems they face. Native cultures, likewise, need to adapt. By adjusting in appropriate ways, they, too, can continue to be a useful force in people's lives. The Iroquois, under Handsome Lake's leadership, is an example of doing so.

3. **Stop substance abuse and cultural apathy: "I will break the cycle of personal and cultural decay by ceasing to be a substance abuser."**

Cultural decline and personal dysfunction often go hand in hand. Among Native people, recovery can be expected to be a dual process that involves cultural renewal coupled with positive, healthy, and functional personal choices. Handsome Lake clearly recognized this truth. Besides merely asking people to rebuild their culture, he also urged them to start new lives by abandoning their dysfunctional habits.

A strong cultural heritage is not all that is needed for recovery. Recovery is hard work and it must be pursued at a very personal level. In situations where substance abuse has been caused by the pain and confusion of cultural disarray, patterns of dysfunctions have a way of building upon themselves. As a result, substance abuse must be attacked as a separate problem regardless of what may have originally caused it.

Although people need to confront their problems without making excuses, it is useful to remember that personal and cultural problems are often related. By keeping this fact in mind, both cultural and personal renewal becomes possible.

4. **Admit to errors made: "I recognize my past errors and I will remember them when choosing a more noble and fulfilling path"**

People make bad choices and these errors need to be recognized. There is an old proverb that says something like, "if people do not know history they are destined to repeat it." That is true both for large countries and for specific people. Those who are not aware of the errors that caused their past failures are likely to make the same mistakes again and again. In Alcoholics Anonymous and its 12 Step Program, for example, alcoholics are urged to become aware of what triggered their alcoholic drinking and work towards recovery with this information clearly in mind.

By centering upon what triggered past troubles, a better toolkit for recovery can be created. And it can be used to pursue a path towards a healthy and permanent sobriety.

5. **Do not repeat errors of the past: "Having chosen a more noble and fulfilling path, I will strive to keep my errors in the past and correct errors and misjudgments as soon as they occur."**

Just as the 12 Step Program centers upon living a good life coupled with sobriety, Handsome Lake was equally concerned with living a moral life and eliminating the lapses of judgment that led to problems in the past. Doing so can help overcome anxiety by reducing regrets, sorrow, and the dysfunctional behavior they can trigger. Living a good life serves both society and the individual.

6. **Heritage and Recovery are Linked. "My heritage and my traditions give me a spirituality. By denying my heritage and my traditions, I am denying my own self and may become vulnerable to relapse. By embracing who I am, I can better succeed in recovery and in life."**

This step is a final culmination of the Path. More than any other, it centers upon the linkages between heritage and recovery. Cultures provide people with traditions, beliefs, attitudes, and values that people need to be healthy, happy, and productive. Character, strength, vulnerability, and spirituality largely reflect the culture of a people.

Spirituality is a key to people's identity and the way they respond to circumstance. When people deny their culture, they deny themselves. People who deny their identity (and their needs) can suffer. This can lead to dysfunctional behavior such as substance abuse. By embracing who you are, you can better succeed both in life and in recovery.

This, in a nutshell, is a narrative description of the Path of Handsome Lake as it is presented in Table 8.1.

Steps One, Two, and Six center upon the culture and the way people relate to it. As we have discussed, many Native people have trouble relating to their culture. When this is true, their culture cannot help them to reduce the pain, fears, and anxieties that can trigger substance abuse. A good relationship to a person's cultural heritage is a vital tool of recovery.

Steps Three, Four, and Five, in contrast, deal with individual people and how they must consider their own actions. These activities are somewhat similar to other programs, such as the 12 step that also focus

Table 8.1.   The Path of Handsome Lake

	Step	Analysis
1. Embrace Tradition	The culture and its value is recognized.	Embracing your culture can provide meaning to life and reduce anxiety
2. Transform Tradition	Cultures must keep up with the times if they are to be strong and effective.	Due to changing times, cultures can lose their ability to help people. Adjusting the culture can restore its ability to help people live fulfilling lives.
3. Stop Abuse/Apathy	To recover, To recover, people must stop substance abuser abuse and quit being apathetic.	No matter what the original cause, substance abuse and apathy become powerful forces that must be combated.
4. Admit Errors	To recover and to be a good member of society, people must admit their past mistakes.	Admitting errors may be hard, but doing so can make it easier to understand why problems developed.
5. Don't Repeat Errors	By admitting past errors, avoiding future mistakes can become easier.	Past errors, painful though they are, provide invaluable clues. These insights are valuable and should be accepted for that reason.
6. A Profound Link	The heritage of the culture and the recovery of the individual are often linked.	The health of the individual and the strength of the culture often go hand in hand. For that reason, programs of recovery need to deal both with the person and the culture.
Discussion	For Native people to recover from dysfunctional behavior, they often need to focus on their culture and their relationship to it. In addition, they need to acknowledge their own behavior and accept responsibility for it. Doing so provides a powerful program of recovery.	

upon acknowledging past mistakes, correcting wrongs, and starting a new way of life.

THE PATH OF HANDSOME LAKE AND ALCOHOLICS ANONYMOUS

The Path of Handsome Lake and the 12 Steps Program of Alcoholics Anonymous/Narcotics Anonymous are similar in many ways. AA and NA, however, do not deal with the health of the culture and the substance abuser's relationship to it. Such issues should not be ignored because they are profoundly important to Native people.

Although the founders of Alcoholics Anonymous did not focus on cultural stress, it is not at odds with the Path of Handsome Lake. It does, however, fail to deal with a number of issues that Native people often need to consider. As a result, while many Native Americans may benefit from Alcoholics Anonymous and Narcotics Anonymous, they may need to focus on other areas, such as the cultural heritage.

Many Native people in recovery will probably participate within Alcoholics Anonymous and Narcotics Anonymous because they are the most popular self-help groups serving substance abusers. As a result of this reality, any and all conflict between Alcoholics Anonymous/Narcotics Anonymous and the Path of Handsome Lake need to be avoided.

MAINTAINING A PROPER FOCUS

While it is useful to recall that Handsome Lake experienced a remarkable recovery from seemingly incurable alcoholism, it is equally important to keep in mind that he had many other achievements as well. Handsome Lake, for example, is the founder of the "Long House" religion that combined long-established Iroquois traditions with other beliefs and attitudes. As is often the case, furthermore, the new ideas of one generation are apt to become the conservative beliefs of the next. Today, for example, the Long

House religion that Handsome Lake established is the faith of the more traditional element of Iroquois society. As such, these people often disagree with the more "liberal" or "progressive" segments of Iroquois society.

I have no interest in entering into any debate regarding the pros and cons of the contemporary Long House religion. I am merely interested in the fact that Handsome Lake recognized that his culture was under profound attack and that he forged a way to preserve his traditions, on the one hand, while adjusting them to circumstance, on the other. Handsome Lake clearly saw a link between a healthy society and personal sobriety. It is possible to focus upon these important considerations and not get caught up in a religious debate.

Handsome Lake provides a valuable strategy for Native people who seek to recover from substance abuse. Because Handsome Lake personally dealt with issues concerning the decay of cultural traditions and the resulting impact upon substance abuse, his path of recovery transcends other programs, such as Alcoholics Anonymous and Narcotics Anonymous that do not deal with cultural stress

Handsome Lake, however, is closely identified with a specific religion that is embraced by a specific segment of Iroquois society. As a result, it is important to avoid partisan religious discussions and focus merely upon his strategy of recovery, a course of action that does not have a specific religious focus.

Handsome Lake saw a profound connection between the decay of his proud Native American culture and the substance abuse experienced by his people. Recognizing this connection, Handsome Lake understood that the recovery of the individual and the viability of the society go hand in hand. While he insisted that while the Iroquois heritage should be embraced, he also recognized that it also must meet the challenges of the times and transform itself. If these adjustments are made, Native substance abusers will be better able to recover.

Chapter 9

Landmarks of the Path

While the Path of Handsome Lake helps Native substance abusers to recover by embracing their culture, The Landmarks of the Path provides a set of guidelines and milestones to follow during this process. The Landmarks are a practical way of applying the Path. The Path and the Landmarks combine to form provide a useful program of recovery that is culturally sensitive.

In chapter 8, a culturally sensitive a tool of recovery was presented. As discussed, Alcoholics Anonymous/Narcotics Anonymous focuses primarily upon the individual and, as a result, they do not focus on cultural matters. These issues, however, are very important to many Native people.

THE LANDMARKS AND THEIR PURPOSE

While the Path of Handsome Lake links personal recovery to cultural health, the Landmarks of the Path, introduces more concrete goals and specific targets of action. The Landmarks do not intended to replace the Path, but they do help people to apply it.

As with the Path of Handsome Lake, The Landmarks of the Path can be presented as a six-step process. These steps include: (1) "We recognize who we are," (2) "We acknowledge that our heritage, culture, and traditions are our strength," (3) "We reject the vulnerability that comes from ignoring our roots," (4) "We realize that others may have their own tradition and we respect them," (5) "We understand that strength that comes from embracing ourselves, not retreating from challenges," (6) "Handsome Lake's example and advice may be useful to all who face personal disruptions."

In this manner, the Landmarks provide a systematic way of addressing the needs of Native substance abusers whose malady is triggered (at least in part) by cultural issues. While not all people will follow the Landmarks in the order in which they are provided, this discussion shows how they can build upon each other in positive and constructive ways.

Having listed these six landmarks, each is discussed with specific reference to the needs of Native substance abusers. These discussions are followed by a concluding statement that discusses how the Path and the Landmarks can be combined in interlocking fashion.

1. **We recognize who we are**

In general, progress in life only comes when people recognize who they are and act in accordance with that reality. People, however, are very complex and are made up of many bits of personality, character, and past experience. Some of these categories may include negative traits (such as a person's vulnerability to alcohol and/or drugs.) Other categories, (such as personal skills and identities) are positive in nature. In order for people to envision who they are, they need a complete and honest vision. In Alcoholics Anonymous and Narcotics Anonymous this process is called "taking an inventory."

People attempt to recover from substance abuse because they (or somebody else) recognize a problem. This realization usually occurs after a number of unfortunate incidents showcase their dysfunctional behavior.

Specific individuals may be saddled with very real shortcomings that prevent them from reaching their goals. Some people have personalities that make their relationships with others difficult. Programs such as the 12 Step program of Alcoholics Anonymous and Narcotics Anonymous, for example, urge participants to reflect on their shortcomings (whatever they may be) in order to understand who they really are. There is no reason to reject that advice.

Some "shortcomings" merely indicate an inability to achieve sought after goals. People often lack the skills or abilities they need to do well, possibly because they lack an education or marketable skills. Others may be held back by ghosts of the past, such as crippling debt, the distrust of others caused by past misdeeds, a criminal record, and so forth. Perhaps age or illness has caused a person to lose the prowess that they once possessed. People need to candidly think about who they are and develop realistic expectations. People who ignore the truth set themselves up to fail.

Besides their shortcomings and limitations, people have strengths and abilities that provide the ability to change their lives for the better. People who have had a string of hard times and disappointments due to drinking and drugging, however, may have trouble recognizing their positive traits and the strength.

In Alcoholics Anonymous, people are often asked to "take their inventory" in a way that acknowledges both assets and liabilities. Doing so can provide a strong foundation for recovery because it forces the person to be realistic.

The cultural heritage provides is another part of who a person is. Even when people do not recognize it, people are often strongly influenced by their cultural origins. By possessing an accurate vision of their own identity, the influences impacting them, and their potentials for the future, people can more effectively meet the challenges of life.

2. **We acknowledge that our heritage, culture, and traditions are our strength.**

Not only do people need to understand who they are and the fact that their heritage is a big part of their identity, they also need to recognize that it can give them strength, power, and purpose. A strong and positive connection with your culture is a powerful asset even though it is often ignored. Forgetting your cultural identity and thinking it has little effect upon you, furthermore, can be very hurtful.

Understood and strengthened who you are. Doing so can prevent you from being blindsided" by failing to understand how you think, feel, and behave.

3. **We reject the vulnerability that comes from ignoring our roots.**

As Native cultures have been drawn into the mainstream world, there has been a tendency for people to ignore their roots. When this occurs, Native people often suffer.

Even when their cultural heritage is important, people might not consciously realize it. This can make people vulnerable. But such vulnerabilities can be overcome if people develop an awareness of their cultural traditions.

Native people need to overcome the danger that comes from ignoring their roots. By affirming their cultural identity (and learning more about their heritage if necessary) people will be better able to connect with who they are. By so doing, Native substance abusers can more effectively cope with the pressures of life

4. **We realize that others may have their own traditions and we respect them.**

Those from different cultures are apt to experience their own feelings, motives, goals, strengths, and weaknesses. This is true in both within the mainstream world and the Native community. Even specific Native traditions (such as the Athabascan) are made up of many subgroups that are distinct.

It is important to develop an appreciation of (and if necessary a tolerance for) the way of life practiced by other people. Overcoming our own prejudice against others is very important.

Other programs of recovery attempt, in their own way, to deal with the fact that people who come from different backgrounds may band together to combat substance abuse. Various Alcoholics Anonymous "folk tales," for example, tell of the respected college professor or sophisticated scientist who learned the basics of recovery from some working class alcoholic who was short of book-learning, but had found a way to stay sober. The moral of such stories is that all substance abusers have similar goals and that people who are very different can help each other.

As far as they go, such ideas are useful. But the opposite observation can also be made. The Handsome Lake program recognizes and celebrates cultural differences and urges its members to value their distinctiveness.

People are products of al background that provides them with a specific way of being human. Others have their own traditions, which are meaningful and powerful to them. Learning about, acknowledging, and celebrating this diversity is important and empowering. And, of course, tolerance and understanding are profoundly valuable skills when people work together for a common goal, such as recovering from substance abuse.

Just as each of us comes from a specific cultural tradition, other people bring their own heritage with them. By creating an open and respectful forum, those seeking recovery can band together in search of sobriety. Instead of ignoring differences or arguing about them, diversity can be celebrated.

5. **We understand that strength comes from embracing ourselves, not retreating from challenges.**

If people are to put their lives in order, they need to accept themselves for who they are. A part of this identity involves the degree to which they fit into the mainstream culture. While the larger world (and people's places within it) may need to be acknowledged and embraced, this represents only a part of personal identity. Aspects of the mainstream world, however, are often more obvious to people than their Native heritage.

Rapid change can be hurtful. I am reminded of the term "future shock" that was coined by Alvin Toffler many years ago. Toffler noted that modern society is in such a rapid state of change that people, raised in one era, must live in another. The differences between these two eras, unfortunately, can be immense. As a result, people become uncomfortable because they must live in a world that is very different from the one in which they were raised. Toffler, of course, was inspired by the anthropological idea of "culture shock" in which people entering a foreign society often face stress, confusion, and dysfunction. Native people are often simultaneously impacted by both future shock and culture shock. Their world is changing quickly and their cultures are often being overpowered by alien ways of life. It should come as little surprise that many Natives exposed to these pressures suffer from substance abuse and other dysfunctions.

By re-embracing their traditions, people can gain the strength they need to meet the problems of life. By accepting who they are, people can better employ the tools that their culture provides and use them to combat their problems.

Substance abuse is often a form of self-medication that is used to deal with the constant crises they face because their cultures are in a state of disarray or because they are not adequately attuned to it. An antidote for these problems is to for people to accept their cultural heritage and not retreat from it.

6. **Handsome Lake's example may be useful to others who face personal disruptions.**

Programs of recovery typically point to the value of helping others. When people are given a second chance in life, they often want to share their good fortune. While they should do so in a non-forceful and non-judgmental manner, helping others is beneficial both to the giver and the receiver.

The Handsome Lake program is built upon developing cultural self-awareness so people can understand who they are, why they respond in the way they do, and how they can overcome their addiction.

Handsome Lake challenged people to live a sober and moral life. He also emphasized that this goal could best be achieved by embracing their heritage. Those seeking recovery can benefit from Handsome Lake's example and the advice he gave. And all people can benefit from acknowledging who they are and by using that reality as a stepping stone towards recovery.

By embracing their cultural heritage and by understanding its impact, recovering alcoholics can gain valuable tools of sobriety. By ignoring their traditions, in contrast, profound triggers to dysfunctional behavior may remain unaddressed and sources of strength will remain untapped.

The Landmarks can be presented in tabular form (see Table 9.1):

The Landmarks of the Path as represented in Table 9.1 emerge as a specific set of strategies that people can employ to rebuild their heritage, affirm their connection to it, and live a productive and fruitful life as they recover from substance abuse. While the Landmarks was not suggested by Handsome Lake, it does provide clues, suggestions, and orientations on how to follow it.

DISCUSSION AND CONCLUSION

The Landmarks of the Path provides (1) a strategy for following the Path of Handsome Lake as well as (2) providing a set of yardsticks by which progress can be evaluated.

Being patterned after the life and work of Handsome Lake (a Native leader who helped his people cope with the trauma caused by social, economic, and political change) the program suggested here is designed to acknowledge and deal with the disruptions that undermine Native cultures as well as the dysfunctional behavior that such disruptions can cause.

While many strategies of recovery seek to treat all substance abusers as if they are identical, this program acknowledges differences between people and their cultures and it encourages people to accept themselves for who they are. Doing so creates a useful way for diverse people to connect with each other in order to combat a common problem, while acknowledging and honoring their distinctiveness.

Table 9.1.   Landmarks of the Path

Landmark	Significance	Discussion
Recognize who we are	People in recovery need to understand their strengths, weaknesses, and identities.	Although AA's 12 Step program focuses on strengths and weaknesses, it does not deal with cultural identities.
Acknowledge power of culture	Recovering people often need to acknowledge their cultural identity and what it impacts.	If people are unaware of their cultural identity, they might not totally understand themselves.
Transcend alienation	When cultures are weakened or ignored, people can become vulnerable to substance abuse. By strengthening these traditions, dysfunction can be overcome.	The dysfunctional behavior resulting form alienation can be reversed by strengthening and embracing the culture.
Respect other traditions	Other people possess cultures and traditions that are meaningful to them. These heritages deserve the respect of others.	Recovery often takes place alongside others from different cultures. Understanding and honoring different cultures is important.
Embrace ourselves	Since cultural identity is a crucial part of personality and character, people need to become consciously aware of it and its power.	By better understanding their personality and character (and their cultural origins), substance abusers can better restructure their lives and recover.
Many can benefit	Because ignoring a cultural identity potentially impacts all people, those from many different cultures can benefit from following the Path of Handsome Lake.	Many people, some more than others, have suffered grievous impacts from rapid cultural change. They can benefit from this program.
Discussion	The Landmarks of the Path provides a means of applying the Path of Handsome Lake. It can also be used to gauge the degree to which progress is being made. It focuses the power and significance of the cultural heritage and it unites people of different traditions while acknowledging their distinctiveness.	

Prologue to Part 4
Different Strategies of Recovery

Now that we have seen how Handsome Lake combines personal recovery with cultural renewal, we need to discuss how the program can actually be applied. In general, programs of recovery can take two different routes. One involves self-help activities. The other employs the use of professional counselors or therapists. These two tools of recovery, of course, are often combined.

Chapter 10 deals with self help programs. The Handsome Lake program can be employed as the primary tool of recovery. Because it does not conflict with other programs, such as Alcoholics Anonymous or Narcotics Anonymous, people can benefit from both. Remember: The Handsome Lake program is better equipped to deal with cultural themes than many other alternatives.

The Handsome Lake program can be used either with lone individuals or within a group context. It can also be employed as a primary program of recovery or serve a supplemental role.

Chapter 10

Handsome Lake and Self-Help

Self-help programs are often a crucial and irreplaceable part of recovery and sobriety. Many self-help programs, however, are not particularly sensitive to cultural issues. The Handsome Lake program, in contrast, can help Native people deal with their heritage, traditions, and culture.

Substance abuse is a major problem in the United States. It afflicts both mainstream and Native people. Self-help is an irreplaceable tool that is used by millions of recovering substance abusers. Here we will discuss how the Handsome Lake program can be used as a self-help activity.

Many Native substance abusers are involved in mainstream self-help programs, such as Alcoholics Anonymous and Narcotics Anonymous that do not deal with cultural issues. These programs are likely to ignore the fact that many Native cultures are under attack and that recovering Natives may be estranged from their heritage.

This chapter focuses upon the value of using the Handsome Lake method within a variety of self-help contexts in order to deal with the cultural aspects of your life. By considering the issues discussed here, you will also be better equipped to deal with the impact of social change. You will also be better able to use your heritage as a tool of recovery.

A PRIMARY PROGRAM

Programs of recovery that embrace the Handsome Lake approach may be used as a primary tool of self-help. This book emphasizes that many Native people are not adequately attuned to their heritage and are unaware of the power that their culture has over them and how it can contribute both to their substance abuse and recovery.

As we have emphasized, many of the more popular self-help programs do not address cultural issues and the pain and vulnerability they create. These programs tend to assume that the culture is strong and vital and that it is not under attack. In reality, the heritage of Native people is often weakened and people are unable to relate to it in a positive manner. The Handsome Lake method is designed to deal with these hurtful situations. It can serve as a primary program of recovery and can be adapted for both individual or group self-help activities.

SETTING THE STAGE

It is very important to remember that cultural decline or alienation from your heritage can trigger substance abuse.

When envisioning the example of Handsome Lake, it is useful to remember that he was a seemingly incurable alcoholic who recovered and become an important leader of the Iroquois people. Those embracing Handsome Lake's program of recovery need to focus on how he combined personal recovery with cultural renewal. Handsome Lake's example of personal success may help you to believe that your own recovery is possible.

Have you been personally hurt by a changing world in which your heritage was ignored and devalued? If so, you might benefit from searching for a possible relationship between these experiences and your substance abuse. The Handsome Lake method can help you do so.

You also need to remember that people are often unaware of their own identity and how it influences their behavior. Understanding these connections is often complicated and difficult, but, the process can be vital to recovery. If possible, write up your own personal history so you can re-read it later in order to recall how you felt at the beginning of your program of recovery. It is truly amazing how quickly people forget what they once felt and experienced. A personal record is probably the only way you can recapture those feelings. (If you do not write very much, even jotting down a few phrases on a topic can help you to jog your memory latter on.)

Various tools may help you understand and reconnect with your heritage. Many Native cultures, for example, publish lists of their values in an attractive format. These lists can be of great value to those engaged in a self-help program of recovery. If you are a member of a Native culture that has compiled such a list, it can provide a useful way of connecting with your heritage. If your culture has not created such a document, the lists provided by other Native peoples may help you remember your own heritage.

As has been emphasized, if a program of recovery does not deal with cultural stress and alienation, it is ill equipped to deal with a major source of Native substance abuse. As a result, Native addicts often need programs and therapies that provide a strong cultural foundation and orientation.

If you practice the Path of Handsome Lake program where a strong Native community exists, you may have access to elders who will help you work towards recovery. Because elders understand their heritage and are committed to passing it on to the next generation, the Handsome Lake program can draws upon their strength and knowledge.

A PRIMARY INDIVIDUAL PROGRAM PRACTICED ALONE

Self-help programs are typically group activities. Many Native people, however, live in fairly remote areas and, therefore, they may not have access to group activities, in general, or the Handsome Lake

program, in specific. If you are in such a situation, you might use the Path of Handsome Lake Program independently.

When working alone, you will not experience the companionship that is often a useful tool of recovery. As a result, you might not have anyone to introduce you to the program. As a result, progress may be painfully slow at first. But by focusing upon the culture and its impact, you can gain many important benefits.

If working alone, you should remain consciously aware of the Path of Handsome Lake and the Landmarks of the Path (and have copies of both posted where you can see them on a daily basis). Other self-help programs you have experienced may have a different focus. If this is true, think about these differences and why they exist. Variations do not mean that either the Handsome Lake program (or any other) is "wrong."

As discussed earlier, the Handsome Lake program deals with culture and traditions and it encourages participants to be conscious of their heritage. Affirming that the heritage and traditions are powerful tools, the Handsome Lake method emphasizes the person's cultural heritage and how it can serve as a foundation for recovery.

Because the culture serves as a source of strength, it can help people overcome substance abuse. If you are comfortable with your culture, the process of a true recovery can be strengthened. As a result, strengthening your culture and feeling that you are a part of it can be vital.

Even when working completely alone, individual primary self-help activities centered on your cultural heritage can help you understand what triggers your substance abuse and how to combat it.

PRIMARY SELF-HELP GROUP ACTIVITIES

As indicated above, individual and independent self-help activities can address your needs, but they take place largely in isolation. Group activities, in contrast, involve contact with other people. Such an arrangement has both benefits and drawbacks. For one thing, self-help groups are run by lay people who probably have little professional training. As a result, these well-meaning individuals may not understand important aspects of substance abuse that might be affecting you. Nonetheless, a group of motivated people working towards their mutual benefit can be helpful and provide strength.

In self-help groups, participants come and go and some members become better versed in the program than others. Nonetheless, everyone tends to be given as "equal voice" and individual participants must figure out for themselves who can provide them with good advice. When employing the Handsome Lake program, a basic consideration is that cultural stress and/or decline (coupled with the possible alienation from a cultural heritage) can trigger substance abuse. By strengthening your culture and building a strong relationship with it, you can develop valuable tools of recovery. Although not all members of self-help groups will be as aware of the program as others, the various steps in the Path of Handsome Lake and the Landmarks of the Path constantly reinforce this theme. In this way, you can focus upon your culture and your relationship to it.

While you need to center upon your own cultural identity, a particular group may have members that derive from different cultural traditions[1] and the needs of all should be addressed. By doing so, everyone can better understand how cultural decline and personal alienation from their heritage might trigger substance abuse.

In programs that are primarily based on the Handsome Lake method, the Native culture and its role in recovery will probably have a central focus. Other self-help programs, such as Alcoholics Anonymous and Narcotics Anonymous, may also be involved. As a result, the Handsome Lake program will often be used in conjunction with other tools of recovery.

A SUPPLEMENTAL SELF-HELP PROGRAM

Well-established methods of recovery, such as Alcoholics Anonymous dominate the self-help community. Unfortunately, typical programs do not deal with cultural stress, decline, and alienation. The Handsome Lake method can be an invaluable supplement to your program of recovery because it does so.

If you use the Path of Handsome Lake program in conjunction with other tools of self help, remember that each program has a different role.

Discussions in self-help meetings can underscore ways in which members identify with the mainstream world vs. their traditional culture. Because these two worlds may be in significant conflict with each other, dealing with these differences can be important to recovery.

SELF-HELP GROUP ACTIVITIES

In self-help activities, the group often has a power that transcends the individual. If used to supplement other programs, the Path of Handsome Lake can deal with cultural issues in a manner that can contribute to recovery.

During meetings, a wide number of participants can probably deal with how their culture and heritage impacts them. When specific examples of cultural stress, conflict, and anxiety are analyzed, they need to be discussed in ways that the entire group can understand.

As has been emphasized, the Handsome Lake method is not in conflict or in competition with any other tools of recovery, and it can serve a unique role by dealing with the cultural traditions and their impacts. In this way, it can serve as a supplemental program of value to many participants.

CONCLUSION

The Handsome Lake self help method can be used in many ways. On some occasions, the method may emerge as the primary self-help activity. In other contexts, it may serve as a supplemental program. As a result, the Handsome Lake program can be applied in at least four distinct ways, (1) individual primary self-help activities, (2) individual supplemental self-help program, (3) Primary group self-help efforts and (4) supplemental self-help group therapy. The unique value of the program is that if focuses upon the individual's culture and its role both in substance abuse and recovery. Various suggestions have been made regarding how to use this valuable and unique program.

NOTE

1.   Even among members of the same Native culture there are often many groups that are unique in their own distinctive ways. Among the Athabascan people of interior Alaska, for example, the culture is made up of many separate tribes. As a result, establishing a self-help group of Native people who are culturally "identical" is almost impossible.

REFERENCES

Fischer, A. R., Jome, L. M., & Atkinson, D. R. (1998). Reconceptualizing multicultural counseling: Universal healing conditions in a culturally specific context. *The Counseling Psychologist, 26*(4), 525-588

Napoleon, H. (1996). *Yuuyaraq: The way of being human.* Fairbanks, AK: Alaska Native Knowledge Network.

Sue, D. W., Arrodondo, P., & McDavis R. J. (1992). Multicultural counseling competencies and standards: A call to the profession. *Journal of Counseling and Development, 70*(4), 477-486.

Chapter 11

Using Counselors and Therapists

Many recovering substance abusers work with professional counselors and therapists. Much professional therapy, however, is designed for mainstream people and might not deal with Native cultural issues. The Handsome Lake Program provides this cultural orientation, and it can be used as a primary tool of recovery or as a supplemental program serving either individuals or groups.

People who seek to recover from substance abuse often work with professional counselors and therapists. This chapter talks about that kind of relationship.

The structure of this chapter is similar to chapter 10. Indeed, some of the information found there is repeated here because you might go directly to this chapter before looking at chapter 10.

Those who are receiving professional treatment may work with counselors or therapists who are familiar with the Handsome Lake program and recommend it. On many occasions, however, your counselor will not be familiar with it. If this is true, the counselor or therapist will need to be made them aware of the Handsome Lake program. In such a situation, you need to be able to say why you believe it can help you.

A word of caution is important here. Although counselors may be willing to try new things, they often have a favorite method. In addition, they might remind you that they are the professionals. Be tactful and respectful when dealing with people who have power over you. In any event, the Handsome Lake program provides a way to deal with your culture and the strengths and vulnerabilities it creates.

In some cases, a Handsome Lake-style of treatment may be employed as the primary tool of therapy. In other cases, a Native-centered program of therapy might emerge as a supplemental means of addressing your needs as a Native person. In either case, acknowledging a Native identity and focusing therapy around can aid in your recovery.

A PRIMARY PROGRAM

It is possible to use the Handsome Lake program as the primary tool of therapy. Doing so can be important because many Native substance abusers are out of touch with their cultural heritage or have not considered how it can contribute to their recovery. If you are such a person, you can benefit from the cultural grounding that the Handsome Lake program provides.

When the Alcoholics Anonymous 12 Step Program (and many other strategies of therapy) was developed, little attention was paid to the pain and sorrow that weakening cultural traditions can cause. These programs tend to assume that the culture is strong and healthy and that substance abusers will be able to reconnect with it once they get their life in order. As a result, the program centers on the individual, not the culture.

This focus creates a blind spot that can be significant because Native people often need to deal with cultural issues. The Path of Handsome Lake program is designed to help you do so. It can be used both in individual counseling and in group therapy.

STRUCTURING THE PROGRAM/SETTING THE STAGE

If you need to deal with cultural decline or a personal alienation from your heritage, the Handsome Lake Program can serve you well.

You might benefit by viewing yourself as a Native person who has been harmed because your heritage was ignored, denied, or devalued. The impact of such hurtful events upon your substance abuse needs to be discussed. The Path of Handsome Lake and the Landmarks of the Path provide a way of doing this important work.

It might also be good for you and your therapist to remember that people are not always conscious of who they really are and what actually influences their behavior. As a result, coming to truly understand yourself may be difficult and take much time and hard work. A good way to start is to complete a number of written assignments that you can share with your counselor. In that way, you will come to sessions with specific things to talk about so conversations will stay focused.

Published lists of the values of particular Native cultures can be valuable tools. If such a list exists for your culture, it can be used to trigger discussions. If not, the lists created by other Native peoples may substitute. Perhaps you and your therapist can invite a respected elder to be a guest at one of your sessions in order to provide insights regarding your cultures and its traditions.

Remember, a program of therapy that does not deal with cultural stress and alienation is often unable to address a major source of Native substance abuse. As a result, you probably need therapy that provides a strong cultural foundation.

In situations where the Handsome Lake program is practiced, a strong Native community may exist. If so, you may have access to elders and others who carry the traditions of your people. Enlisting the aid of these cultural leaders can be an important aspect of recovery. You might also want to find out if local Native recovery programs emphasize the Native culture. If so, perhaps they have valuable tools and resources you can embrace.

Many Native people are aware of the importance of their culture and how it can help people overcome the problems in their lives. Many Native programs of recovery seek to connect with the cultural traditions of participants so they can use their heritage as a tool of recovery. This book provides a structure for doing so.

In any event, your program of recovery probably needs to acknowledge your Native cultural heritage. Conflicts between the Native and mainstream cultures also need to be considered. By addressing these issues, you can begin to see what has been lost as Native cultures have been weakened and/or as you have drifted away from your heritage.

PRIMARY INDIVIDUAL COUNSELING

Individual counseling, by nature, is a "one on one" activity involving you and a counselor working together, largely in isolation. Although some group sessions with other people may occasionally take place, individual therapy largely involves a strong relationship between the counselor and the client. This arrangement possesses both strengths and weaknesses that stem from the self-contained nature of the relationship. Thus, individual counseling can be closely attuned to your special needs. In order to receive these individualized benefits, however, therapy lacks the valuable inputs a group can provide. The isolation of individual therapy, however, can protect you from the possible shame and humiliation that might occur is you were asked to admit to certain past misdeeds within a group setting.

Another difference is that in group therapy newcomers may be able to "pick up" the essentials of the program by watching and listening to others and by being coached by them. In individual therapy, in contrast, you and the therapist may need time to learn the basics of the program. Under these circumstances, just "getting the ball rolling" can be a painfully slow process. A useful alternative is for you to be involved in some kind of group counseling or self-help activities that deal with the Handsome Lake method. In this way, you can learn the essentials of the method from the group; this can speed up your progress because individual counseling sessions will not have to deal with basic issues.

In any event, you need to be consciously aware of the Path and the Landmarks (and you should have copies of both) in order to be reminded of the program and how it works. If you have been previously involved in substance abuse therapy, you might have prior experience with other programs and have pre-conceptions about what to expect. If so, you need to remember that the Handsome Lake program is different because it is deeply concerned with your cultural heritage. It points to cultural renewal as a key to recovery. Emphasizing that recovery is linked to a strong and vibrant cultural heritage, the Path of Handsome Lake centers upon how you can benefit from connecting with your heritage in strong and personal ways.

As argued above, your cultural heritage, when functioning properly, can serve as a source of comfort and strength. It can protect you against stress and anxiety. Your cultural heritage can also serve as a powerful means of controlling the pain that can lead to substance abuse. But if you cannot identify with your culture or if it is weakened, it will not be able to provide this comfort and protection.

By strengthening your culture and by becoming comfortable with it, you can gain powerful tools of recovery.

Individual therapy is often the most effective way to explore how your substance abuse began. It can also be used to understand the impact of your culture upon your behavior. In individual therapy, you will be in a position to deal with personal issues in a private context that protects you from making embarrassing admissions in a public.

PRIMARY GROUP THERAPY

As indicated above, individual "one on one" counseling has the advantage of focusing upon your special needs and doing so in private. This isolation can be both a strength and a weakness. Group therapy, in contrast, is able to provide the multiple perspectives. In addition, groups often develop an identity of their own that has a significant therapeutic value. Because of its interpersonal dynamics, group therapy is often more powerful and effective than individual counsel-

ing. I have no opinion regarding what is right for you. But I do know that both individual and group therapies have their own distinctive roles, strengths, and weaknesses. And, as indicated above, group and individual therapy can often work together in positive ways that build upon each other.

Some groups are ongoing, although specific group members may come and go over time. Where this is true, knowledge of the Path of Handsome Lake/Landmarks of the Path will become a feature of that group. Where the group is permanent and ongoing, existing members can orient newcomers and make them aware of the basics of the program. This can save you time and effort when you first join. Some groups, in contrast, are created for a special purpose and they have a limited life span. When such a group is begun, it may be necessary for all or most members to learn about the Handsome Lake program and how it works. During these early sessions, you can expect the therapist to provide more leadership and control until the members understand the program.

Everyone in the group, including yourself, needs to clearly understand how the Handsome Lake program works, why it is structured the way it is, and what it seeks to accomplish. As emphasized above, when cultures are weakened and when people are distanced from them, the potential for substance abuse may arise. By rebuilding the strength of the culture and your connection to it, you can gain valuable tools of recovery. As a result of this progress, you can become better equipped to lead a fruitful and sober life.

A part of this process can involve a more complete and positive introduction (or re-introduction) to your Native culture. The goal is to help you connect (or reconnect) with your heritage in a positive way. A particular therapy group, however, will probably be composed of members of various Native cultures; as a result, therapy cannot merely focus upon your culture.[1] Instead, you can expect a program that is designed to help all members of the group to recognize the power of their own particular cultural heritage. In the process, each member, including yourself, can better understand how cultural decline and personal alienation from your heritage might have triggered substance abuse.

While the Handsome Lake method may dominate in some situations or be the only tool of therapy that is being employed, on other occasions it will be used alongside other therapies. Because other programs are more firmly established, this will commonly occur.

A SUPPLEMENTAL PROGRAM

In reality, of course, other methods of recovery tend to dominate substance abuse therapy. And the most prevalent method is the 12 Step Program developed by Alcoholics Anonymous. There is a good chance that you will be involved in such a program. Nevertheless, as we have seen, these mainstream programs do not focus upon the vulnerability of Native cultures and the fact that clients may be distanced from their heritage.

The 12 Step Program of Alcoholics Anonymous and Narcotics Anonymous is not designed to deal with the impact of culture upon substance abuse and recovery. They deal with the culture as strong, permanent, and ongoing. Many Native cultures, however, have been significantly undermined and/or people have become distanced from their heritage. The Handsome Lake program deals with these issues. As a result, the Handsome Lake program can be an invaluable supplement to conventional therapy.

When the Handsome Lake program is being used in conjunction with some other program of recovery, you need to remain conscious of the similarities and differences in each program and how they can usefully supplement the other. You need to remember that there is no real conflict between these programs, although each has a different focus.

It is important for you to remember that the mainstream and the Native cultures may be in significant conflict with each other. As a result, when you live in both cultures tensions that cause stress and pain can arise.

INDIVIDUAL SUPPLEMENTAL COUNSELING

Individual supplemental counseling has the same strengths and weaknesses as primary individual counseling (see discussion above). It centers on your unique needs in a focused way, while sacrificing the benefits of group participation.

In individual supplemental counseling, it is vital to determine is some issues are best addressed by the Handsome Lake program while others may be dealt with using another type of therapy. As indicated above, the 12 Step Program does not deal with cultural stress/cultural decline nor does it deal with the possibility that people have become alienated from their heritage. If possible, written assignments prepared outside of the therapy session as "homework" can help you think about these issues.

Your goal should be to determine how the Handsome Lake method and other therapies can contribute to your recovery. What benefits will you get from each? How can these therapies be combined in a fruitful way?

SUPPLEMENTAL GROUP THERAPY

In group therapy, as indicated above, the group has an existence that transcends the individual. Because conventional therapy does not deal with cultural issues, the Handsome Lake program may provide a useful supplemental role. When this is the case, the members will probably come from a number of different backgrounds. These differences need to be taken into account.

During sessions, all the group members will be able to share various aspects of their cultural heritage and the pressures and stresses that their culture faces or has faced. They will also discuss anxieties, fears, and sorrows that have been triggered by cultural stress and/or individual alienation from a cultural heritage. When specific examples of cultural stress, conflict, and anxiety are analyzed, they can be discussed in general terms so all group members can relate to them. Nevertheless, the specifics of particular cases need to be recognized.

It is important to emphasize that the Handsome Lake method is not in conflict or in competition with any other strategy of recovery. Although the distinctiveness of different cultures needs to be emphasized, the fact that diverse cultures may be subjected to similar pressures might emerge as a thread that ties different stories and experiences together.

CONCLUSION

While the Handsome Lake model provides a specific means of therapy, it can be used in a variety of ways.

On some occasions, the method may emerge as the primary vehicle of therapy while, on other occasions, it may serve in a supplemental program. As a result, the Handsome Lake program can be applied in four distinct ways, (1) individual primary therapy, (2) individual supplemental therapy, (3) group primary therapy, and (4) group supplemental therapy. By providing guidelines for each use, the flexibility of the program has been demonstrated.

In view of the fact that the Handsome Lake program is designed to deal with the culture of the individual and how this heritage can be a source of trauma that leads to substance abuse, it can provide a valuable service. In addition, since the cultural heritage can be a source of strength, it needs to be nurtured in order to serve those seeking recovery.

NOTE

1. Even among members of the same Native culture there are often many groups that are unique in their own distinctive ways. Among the Athabascan people of Alaska, for example, the culture is made up of many subsets each having their own traditions and distinctions. As a result, finding a group of Native people who are "identical" is almost impossible.

REFERENCES

Fischer, A. R., Jome, L. M., & Atkinson, D. R. (1998). Reconceptualizing multicultural counseling: Universal healing conditions in a culturally specific context. *The Counseling Psychologist, 26*(4), 525-588.

Napoleon, H. (1996). *Yuuyaraq: The way of being human.* Fairbanks, AK: Alaska Native Knowledge Network.

Sue, D. W., Arrodondo, P., & McDavis R. J. (1992). Multicultural Counseling competencies and standards: A call to the profession. *Journal of Counseling and Development, 70*(4), 477-486.

Appendix

The Path and Landmarks in Poster Form

Those who employ the Handsome Lake method need to keep reminded of the framework that is provided by the Path and the Landmarks. In order to make it easier to keep the program in mind, I am providing statements of both of these tools in poster form. It is hoped that those using the program will photocopy these posters and put them in a prominent place so the principles of the program can be kept in mind.

The Path of Handsome Lake

1. I possess a culture and a tradition. Embracing them is sacred, meaningful, and joyful.

2. All cultural traditions change and all cultural traditions are under attack. I will strive to help my culture evolve and flourish.

3. I will break the cycle of personal and cultural decay by ceasing my substance abuse.

4. I recognize my past errors and I will remember them when choosing a more noble and fulfilling path.

5. Having chosen a more noble and fulfilling path, I will strive to keep my errors in the past and correct errors and misjudgments as soon as they occur.

6. My heritage and my traditions give me a spirituality. By denying my heritage and my traditions, I deny my own self and may become vulnerable to relapse. By embracing who I am, I can better succeed in recovery and in life.

The Landmarks of the Path

1. We recognize who we are.

2. We acknowledge that our heritage, culture, and traditions are our strength.

3. We reject the vulnerability that comes from ignoring our roots.

4. We realize that others may have their own tradition and we respect them.

5. We understand that strength comes from embracing ourselves, not retreating from challenges.

6. Handsome Lake's example and advice may be useful to all who face personal disruptions.

Notes

NOTES

NOTES